M000265863

Body Problems

Body Problems addresses the relationship between the body and society in a fast-food culture. Agger focuses on issues of food, exercise, work, dieting and eating disorders, fashion, bariatric and cosmetic surgery, and health. He addresses a growing, fundamental dilemma that we have ample access to abundant calories yet lead lifestyles and have jobs that for the most part do not enable us to expend those calories. He proposes solutions, both individual and structural, that involve re-orienting ourselves to exercise as play.

This second edition has been updated to include a new chapter on food capitalism and a concluding passage arguing Cartesian dualism can be resolved by exercising vegans in ways that would thwart this food capitalism and give people immense control over their bodies, health, and well-being. The book is ideal for courses in introductory sociology, social problems, work, sociology of sport and leisure, gender, and health and illness.

Ben Agger (1952–2015) was Professor of Sociology and Humanities and Director of the Center for Theory at The University of Texas at Arlington. Among his last published books were *Texting Toward Utopia: Kids, Writing, and Resistance* (2013) and *Oversharing: Presentations of Self in the Internet Age* (2012).

Framing 21st Century Social Issues

Series Editor: France Winddance Twine, University of California, Santa Barbara

The goal of this new, unique series is to offer readable, teachable "thinking frames" on today's social problems and social issues by leading scholars. These are available for view on https://www.routledge.com/Framing-21st-Century-Social-Issues/book-series/SOCISS

For instructors teaching a wide range of courses in the social sciences, the Routledge *Social Issues Collection* now offers the best of both worlds: originally written short texts that provide "overviews" to important social issues *as well as* teachable excerpts from larger works previously published by Routledge and other presses.

As an instructor, click to the website to view the library and decide how to build your custom anthology and which thinking frames to assign. Students can choose to receive the assigned materials in print and/or electronic formats at an affordable price.

Available

Body Problems, Second Edition
Running and Living Long in a Fast-Food Society
Ben Agger

Trans* Lives in the United States
Challenges of Transition and Beyond
Andrew Rene Cutler-Seeber

Entrepreneurs and the Search for the American Dream
Zulema Valdez

The Global Beauty Industry
Colorism, Racism, and the National Body
Meeta Rani Jha

Series Advisory Board: Rene Almeling, *Yale University*, Joyce Bell, *University of Pittsburgh*, Elizabeth Bernstein, *Barnard College*, David Embrick, *Loyola University – Chicago*, Tanya Golash-Boza, *University of California – Merced*, Melissa Harris, *New York University*, Matthew Hughey, *University of Connecticut*, Kerwin Kaye, *SUNY – Old Westbury*, Wendy Moore, *Texas A&M*, Alondra Nelson, *Columbia University*, Deirdre Royster, *New York University*, Zulema Valdez, *University of California – Merced*, Victor Rios, *University of California – Santa Barbara*.

For a full list of titles in this series, please visit https://www.routledge.com/Framing-21st-Century-Social-Issues/book-series/SOCISS

Body Problems

Running and Living Long in a Fast-Food Society

Second Edition

Ben Agger

NEW YORK AND LONDON

Second edition published 2020
by Routledge
52 Vanderbilt Avenue, New York, NY 10017

and by Routledge
2 Park Square, Milton Park, Abingdon, Oxon, OX14 4RN

Routledge is an imprint of the Taylor & Francis Group, an informa business

First edition by Routledge, 2011

Library of Congress Cataloging-in-Publication Data
A catalog record has been requested for this book

ISBN: 978-1-138-65874-5 (hbk)
ISBN: 978-1-138-65875-2 (pbk)
ISBN: 978-1-315-62060-2 (ebk)

Typeset in Garamond and Gill Sans
by Apex CoVantage, LLC

Contents

Contents

Series Foreword

The world in the early 21st century is beset with problems—a troubled economy, global warming, oil spills, religious and national conflict, poverty, human immuno-deficiency virus (HIV), health problems associated with sedentary lifestyles. Virtually no nation is exempt, and everyone, even in affluent countries, feels the impact of these global issues.

Since its inception in the 19th century, sociology has been the academic discipline dedicated to analyzing social problems. It is still so today. Sociologists offer not only diagnoses; they glimpse solutions, which they then offer to policy makers and citizens who work for a better world. Sociology played a major role in the civil rights movement during the 1960s in helping us to understand racial inequalities and prejudice, and it can play a major role today as we grapple with old and new issues.

This series builds on the giants of sociology, such as Weber, Durkheim, Marx, Parsons, and Mills. It uses their frames, and newer ones, to focus on particular issues of contemporary concern. These books are about the nuts and bolts of social problems, but they are equally about the frames through which we analyze these problems. It is clear by now that there is no single correct way to view the world, but only paradigms, models, which function as lenses through which we peer. For example, in analyzing oil spills and environmental pollution, we can use a frame that views such outcomes as unfortunate results of a reasonable effort to harvest fossil fuels. "Drill, baby, drill" sometimes involves certain costs as pipelines rupture and oil spews forth. Or we could analyze these environmental crises as inevitable outcomes of our effort to dominate nature in the interest of profit. The first frame would solve oil spills with better environmental protection measures and clean-ups, while the second frame would attempt to prevent them altogether, perhaps shifting away from the use of petroleum and natural gas and toward alternative energies that are "green."

These books introduce various frames such as these for viewing social problems. They also highlight debates between social scientists who frame problems differently. The books suggest solutions, both on the macro and micro levels. That is, they suggest what new policies might entail, and they also identify ways in which people, from the ground level, can work toward a better world, changing themselves and their lives and families and providing models of change for others.

Readers do not need an extensive background in academic sociology to benefit from these books. Each book is student-friendly in that we provide glossaries of terms for the uninitiated that are keyed to bolded terms in the text. Each chapter ends with questions for further thought and discussion. The level of each book is accessible to undergraduate students, even as these books offer sophisticated and innovative analyses.

Preface

For the first time in human history, people in affluent western societies have enough to eat, and yet their lifestyles, including diet, reliance on the automobile, and desk jobs pose health risks. For millennia before, the most urgent risk was starvation. Thanks to Henry Ford's system of mass production, we not only manufacture cars but also grow food in such abundance that the horn of plenty has become a threat to public and personal health. Body sciences and body industries have arisen in order to meet the challenge of healing people who have too much of a good thing. But I contend that our body problems are best resolved by exercise, especially running.

In this book, I examine the strange fact that we did not identify body problems until the dawn of the modern age; desk jobs and the invention of exercise during the 1970s; body sciences such as medicine and single-number indicators of health and illness; body industries such as gyms, weight-loss programs, and fashion; the first and second running revolutions, the tribe called the Tarahumara, ultramarathoners and transcontinental runners; and, finally, 'slowmodernity'—a blend of healthy lifestyles from pre-industrial cultures and modern benefits such as literacy, technology, medicine, and democracy. Above all, I ask how people can live healthier, less stressful, and more meaningful lives by healing the split between their minds and bodies.

Introduction, Second Edition

What's a Body to Do?

Scott G. McNall

Ben Agger (1952–2015)

I want to introduce readers to the author of this book, Ben Agger, who died unexpectedly on July 14, 2015, of a sudden viral illness. No one anticipated his death because he was in exceptional physical condition. As his wife, Beth Anne Shelton, noted, Ben got up every morning at 3:00 a.m. to run, sometimes long distances, usually upwards of 60 miles a week. He loved to run, as you will learn from the chapters that follow. He ran, not just for the obvious health benefits, but because it gave him a sense of freedom. He speaks, in fact, of running to freedom. Running to something implies running away from something. When he was in the "zone," he ran free from what he characterizes as the corrosive and unhealthy aspects of life in a capitalist world, free from domination, free from the commercial protein, fat, and carbohydrates that make up much of the American diet.

Ben grew up in the running capital of America, Eugene, Oregon. In the 1960s and 1970s Eugene was also a center for political activism, social justice movements, and back to the land movements, where people grew their own food and lived more simply. The first "teach-in" against the war in Vietnam was held at the University of Oregon. Ben carried the optimistic spirit of his hometown throughout his entire career, always hoping that the egalitarian ethos of the 1960s and 1970s could be recovered, if only we understood how the world in which we lived worked. He went to Canada for both his undergraduate degree (York) and his PhD (Toronto) and honed there his understanding of critical theorists such as Marx and members of the Frankfurt School such as Adorno and Horkheimer. Like the theorists he studied, he turned his critical eye on all aspects of modern capitalist society. Ben wrote about everything: the family, schools, jobs, the media, gun culture, neo-liberal capitalism, the 1960s, food, and running.

He also understood that we needed more than to just understand the world; we needed to change it. How? is the question that has bedeviled many critical theorists seeking a place to stand in opposition to an over-rationalized, over-bureaucratized, capitalist society. How can we make a difference when our daily lives are enmeshed in a system of complete domination? One answer is that we start with those things we can control: our bodies, for example.

The topics of diet and the body and its relationship to freedom emerged as a central focus of Ben's recent writing. As a critical food theorist, he both critiqued and sought transformation of agribusiness, school lunch programs, federal farm subsidies, nutrition, and health care. His intention was to write an expanded version of *Body Problems*, adding three additional chapters. He finished two of them, which are included in this new edition. One deals with the virtues of a vegan diet for runners and the other deals with the fact that capitalism makes us sick with processed food and then "heals" us for a quick profit. The chapter he did not finish was going to be about food radicalism in the U.S. from the founding of the restaurant Chez Panisse in Berkeley, California by Alice Waters in 1971, to the work of writers like Michael Pollan who argue that our health depends on eating locally sourced food cooked at home. Pollan and Waters and many others stand in stark opposition to unsustainable corporate agriculture that allows us to eat cheaply but not well, while destroying the environment in the process. I believe we can anticipate from the rest of the book and Ben's other writings what the essence of this chapter would have been. It would have argued, like the chapters on diet and running, that one of the ways for us to take control of our lives is to take control of our bodies, to be mindful of how we eat and live. This is also a step toward creating a sense of community among those who need and wish to overcome the pain and toxicity of modern life. We run to protest capitalist food systems and we run toward freedom. We need to get started.

A Sick Nation

We're a sick nation and getting sicker. A study (2015) by the Nobel Prize-winning economist Angus Deaton and his wife and colleague, Anne Case, observed that white middle-aged Americans (45 to 54 years of age) are dying faster than their counterparts in any other developed nation. Our life expectancy is actually decreasing compared to other countries. Mortality rates for middle-aged Americans are double (more than 400 per 100,000) those of Sweden (about 200 per 100,000). Why are we so sick?

Drawing on data from the Centers for Disease Control and Prevention (CDC), Deaton and Case conclude that middle-aged whites increasingly report mental-health problems and problems in coping with daily life. The rising death rate among 45–54 year-olds is accounted for by an increase in drug and alcohol overdoses, suicides, chronic liver diseases, and diabetes. (The diabetes is a direct outcome of cheap food we eat, which is high in fat and carbohydrates.) Another reason for an increase in death rates is economic stress. Pain and hopelessness can lead to suicide. For many middle-aged and middle-class Americans, the American Dream has ended, and the data suggest things may get worse.

It is unlikely that diseases of despair are going to decline anytime soon. In fact, quite the opposite is occurring. According to data from the CDC, from 2015 to 2016 there was a 28 percent increase in opioid deaths and a 21 percent increase from drugs such as cocaine and methamphetamine. Likewise, deaths from alcohol and suicides increased during this same time span (Bernstein and Ingraham 2017). Why have rates continued to increase when the economy is supposed to have improved, and rates of employment are at an all-time high? There are several things that contribute to a collective sense of despair among those not insulated from economic shocks.

First, the way employment data is reported understates the number of people working full time and, hence, the health of the economy. Those who have given up looking for work are not counted, as well as those too sick to work. Conversely, everybody who works, whether full-time or part-time, are counted as employed, even though many report they want a full-time job (U.S. Department of Labor 2018).

Second, when the economy rebounded after 2008 it deepened the divide between Americans. Those who suffered the loss of work when the automobile industry collapsed, was bailed out, and then downsized, seldom found jobs that paid what they previously earned at General Motors, Ford, or Chrysler. If they were lucky, they found jobs paying $12–15 an hour—not enough to support a family and pay for a mortgage. After 2008, a number of previous homeowners became renters or became homeless along with their children (Goldstein 2018). Between 2008 and 2011 25 percent of all Americans lost 75 percent of all their wealth—their homes, the money they were saving to send children to college, and their modest retirement funds. When the rebound finally began in 2013, the gains in wealth and income went to the top 1 percent, while working Americans were left to scoop up any loose change that was left on the table (Pfeffer, Danziger, and Schoeni 2013).

Finally, the ballyhooed tax breaks for the "middle class" pushed through by Congress in late 2017 further increased the wealth-income gap between Americans. While the legislation was sold with the idea that cutting corporate taxes would spur companies to expand their businesses and hire more employees, they did something else with their windfall. As *The Wall Street Journal* has reported on more than one occasion, corporations used their windfalls to buy back their own stocks, thereby increasing the value of those stocks for shareholders. It also increased the paychecks of chief executives, whose compensation was tied to the performance of their company's stock (Rapoport and Francis 2018). Needless to say, unless you had a robust stock portfolio, you were unlikely to benefit from these tax cuts. As for wage increases, toward the end of 2018, they averaged about 3 percent. To put this in perspective: if you were making $15.00 an hour, you got a raise of 45 cents an hour, or 30 cents, if you were making $10 an hour. This is not much of a windfall for the average wage earner and even this small amount was eaten up by inflation, which hovered at about 3 percent (Kiernan 2018). This inflation was driven in large part by a sharp upturn in the national debt, which was in turn caused by $1 trillion in tax breaks that went to the 1 percent and to corporate America. In short, there are solid reasons for increased despair.

Loss of Autonomy and Freedom

Social factors enter into the equation for the poor health of Americans. As Deaton and Case note, over the last twenty years those with a high-school degree or less saw a four-fold increase in death by drug and alcohol poisoning, a rise in suicide rates by 81 percent, and a 50 percent increase in deaths due to liver disease. The epidemiologist Michael Marmot argues in *The Health Gap* (2015) that poor health can be attributed to a lack of autonomy, empowerment, and freedom. Economic inequality in the United States thus contributes to suicide, heart disease, lung disease, obesity, and diabetes in part because it leads to a feeling that people have no control over their own lives. Being shut out of your own society on the basis of factors you cannot control (for example, whether you were born to rich or poor parents, black or white) leads to poor health. Growing numbers of Americans feel their own society has passed them by.

An Epidemic of Hopelessness

Numerous polls conducted in the run-up to the 2016 presidential election revealed deep anger about the political system and deep pessimism about the economy among the American electorate. This anger and distrust crossed party lines and led to support for candidates like Donald Trump on the right and Bernie Sanders on the left. One poll (O'Connor and Hook 2015) found that 42 percent of Democrats and 35 percent of Republicans felt the political system was rigged in favor of insiders. The same poll revealed that while only 12 percent of Democrats felt out of place in their own country, 45 percent of Republicans did. Another poll (Lauter 2015) found that 70 percent of potential voters felt the country was headed in the wrong direction, even though the unemployment rate had dropped to 5 percent, the lowest level since the financial crisis of 2008. Many Americans hold a dim view of capitalism. Fifty-five percent think the rich are getting richer and the poor, poorer, and 65 percent think most big businesses have dodged taxes, bought favors, and polluted the environment. And only

14 percent of Americans think the next generation will be richer, safer, and healthier than the last one (Montgomerie 2015). The Dream is over.

Healing Ourselves in the Wrong Way

People fight back against a system they feel is out of control in unusual and sometimes destructive ways. Instead of trying to fix the political and economic system that causes us to be on the outside looking in, and instead of trying to change the corporate food system that makes us fat, we look for quick fixes of our bodies. And these fixes are offered by those who profit from them. As Agger notes in this work, we try to reshape our bodies to be more desirable and attractive by dieting, which focuses on the wrong problem. We should instead focus on how to live long and healthy lives. Doctors, insurance companies, and even the government thinks we need to lose weight; however, only a few doctors truly emphasize sensible diets and exercise as a way of getting healthy. That's not where the profit is.

The diet industry is a $60 billion a year business. We spend money trying to lose pounds by joining weight-loss programs, buying gym memberships, and drinking diet sodas that have no nutritional value. As for gym memberships, they spike upwards in January after the holidays and then plummet about a month later. Agger simply urges us to eat good food, run, jog, or walk. For those who join weight-loss programs or decide to follow one of the fad diets, the failure rate runs from 75 to 90 percent (Smith 2015). But if one diet fails, there is always another one just around the corner.

It's not easy to rewire our food tastes. When a diet comes along that suggests we can have it all— or at least the really tasty bits—people jump on it. The Atkins diet, created by the M.D. Robert Atkins (1972), was a big hit with dieters. All you needed to do was cut out the carbohydrates and eat a diet made up almost exclusively of meat, poultry, cheese, butter, fish, and eggs with very few fruits or vegetables. You could also (and still can) order food made to order for your diet. You can order online Atkins' chocolate shakes, chocolate caramel-mousse bars, fudge brownies, and chocolate light meal bars, as well as peanut butter cups. This is a bad diet; it can lead to kidney disease, type 2 diabetes, as well as heart disease. However, this diet has now come around in a new form with two best-selling books by physicians. In *Grain Brain* (2013), David Perlmutter argues against foods consumed throughout human history—corn, rice, and potatoes— leaving us, again, with meat, fish, dairy, and eggs. William Davis (2014) in *Wheat Belly* argues that our way to health is to avoid carbohydrates, wheat, and sugar by eating meat and dairy products.

The claims made for these diets are remarkable, and are built on fear. Perlmutter (2013) claims that eating carbohydrates, even healthy ones like whole grains, can cause "dementia, ADHD [attention deficit hyperactivity disorder], anxiety, chronic headaches, depression, and much more." He says that to have healthy brains we need fat and cholesterol. Take just one of the diseases supposedly "caused" by eating carbs: dementia. It's a frightening disease because it affects about one in ten of the elderly, and there is no cure. Imagine, then, that you or a loved one is suffering from dementia, or you are worried about your own chances of developing symptoms. Along comes a diet that promises to reverse the symptoms and/or prevent them in the first place. According to Perlmutter, "there is no better trio of items to fight Alzheimer's and dementia than grass-fed beef, avocados, and coconut oil." (Science does not support this claim.).

We seem intent on rejecting both science and common sense when it comes to our own bodies. We reject the common-sense notion that we can lead healthier lives if we understand how to use our bodies, because it is too much trouble. Having Jenny Craig ship you food is so much easier. We reject science because many of us have come to believe that science is simply another "opinion," and our "opinion" is just as valid, or even better, when it comes to our bodies.

The shelves of our local grocery stores are now stocked with products labeled "gluten free." There is even gluten-free beer and vodka! There is a big market for these products because many people are overweight and tired and attribute their poor health to intolerance to gluten. Gluten is found in all products made with wheat, as well as many other grains. Yet, as the Celiac Disease Foundation (2018) notes, at *most* only 1 percent of the American population has celiac disease or is gluten intolerant, though many more think they have the disease. Those who stop eating wheat products report feeling better when they go on a gluten-free diet. If they have been eating lots of junk food containing gluten and refined carbohydrates, and stop, they will no doubt feel better. But they also need to limit the amount of red meat, butter, and dairy they eat.

As Agger notes, one of the unhealthier things we do in relationship to our bodies is to accept others' ideas of what constitutes attractiveness. Caught up in the corporate ideas about how our bodies should be clothed, we waste money on trying to be fashionable. Major youth-oriented stores like Kohl's, Abercrombie & Fitch, Urban Outfitters, and Forever 21 depend on young people buying new outfits every year. Even worse, we carve up our bodies to try to meet the demands of the advertising industry and Hollywood's version of how to look. Plastic surgery for cosmetic purposes is a multi-billion-dollar business. In 2016, close to 17 million people underwent some procedure; most were between the ages of 40–54. Women sought to augment their breasts, reshape their noses, reduce their thighs through liposuction, get a facelift, and either reduce the size of their buttocks or enhance their size with an implant. Men got pectoral implants and hair implants (American Society of Plastic Surgeons 2018).

So, what is a body to do? When our body images are shaped by the cosmetic and plastic surgery industries, and what goes into our bodies is for the most part determined by corporate agriculture, where does freedom lie? How do we take control of our own bodies and stand in opposition to a dominant culture that is physically and psychologically harmful? What we put into our bodies and how we shape our bodies has become part of a larger discussion about the need to reject all forms of both government and corporate control over our bodies and lives. There is a common theme that runs through the critical food movement, movements opposed to vaccination, those who want to get genetically modified organisms (GMOs) out of the food chain, and those who believe that corporations are preventing people from gaining access to medicines that could heal them.

The overarching theme here is suspicion of modern science, because movement leaders argue that scientists are simply shills for corporations and therefore can't be trusted (McNall 2018). Food scientists are clear that genetically modified food, for example, corn, wheat, soy, potatoes, and sugar beets, cause no more harm to the human beings who eat them than the "natural" kinds. But this is irrelevant to anti-GMO forces. They oppose GMOs not only for perceived health reasons but because they are taking a stand against the corporatization of everyday life: not just what we eat and what goes into our bodies, but a condemnation of the larger system of capitalism. The anti-GMO movement is ultimately a fight about our bodies and who has a right to control them and that is not corporate America. I believe Ben would agree that it is your right to control your own body and that you need to assert that right.

The anti-vaccination movement (Biss 2014) is similar but stands as an example of harmful ways to take control. Autism is a frightening disease because neither the causes nor the cures are clear. For those parents who "learned" in 1997 that the cause of their child's autism was the mercury in the vaccines their child received, it seemed clear that childhood vaccinations needed to be halted or modified. The paper claiming this link was published in the prestigious British medical journal, *The Lancet,* by Andrew Wakefield, a British doctor. The paper was completely discredited and retracted from the journal and, eventually, Wakefield lost his medical license (Public Health 2015). The CDC has taken the strong position that vaccinations are safe, and notes that a form of mercury never harmful to humans (ethylmercury) was taken out of all childhood vaccines in 2001.

Nevertheless, sites like Health Impact News (2015) accuse the CDC of hiding data proving that mercury in vaccines is linked to autism. The blogs and arguments posted about vaccination revolve around taking a stand against the corporate drug industry that, it is argued, always seeks profits over the safety of people.

Why do so many people follow destructive courses of action, not based in science? It is partly because the current economic system does not give them hope for their immediate or long-term future. Trust in government institutions and the corporate sector, including the corporate medicine and drug industries, is at an all-time low. Taking a stand against what is understood as corporate greed and domination doesn't have to be anti-science; it can be taking a stand for freedom. Ben's argument is that there are good and simple ways to stand in opposition to the world in which we live and to create a community of like-minded others. I know what he would think of the millions who spend hours a day on social media sites and what his advice to them would be: run!

1: There was no Body Problem until Modernity

Descartes, Henry Ford, Corn Syrup, Highways

Sociologists have done excellent work in bringing to light the hidden injuries of our society, from racism and sexism to pollution and global warming. C. Wright Mills (1959) described **sociology** as the discipline that translates a person's private troubles into public issues, in this extending the influence of Marx, Weber, and Durkheim before him. All of these thinkers reflected on the fact that much of what we 'are,' and who we are, depends on our places in society; we are products of social structures and social forces, to use the discipline's jargon.

However, sociologists sometimes miss important emerging issues, either because they take them for granted or because they are late-breaking news. There is little written on the sociology of childhood and children, who could be viewed as a forgotten minority group. And sociologists have tended to ignore bodies as legitimate topics of social-science concern (but see O'Neill 1987). To be sure, scholars in other disciplines, all the way from medicine to women's studies, have studied bodies. And even sociologists have examined food (Glassner 2007) and sports (Carrington and McDonald 2009). Other sociologists have addressed the automobile, highways, cities, factories, offices, and recreation—all of which are topics of my concern.

I am developing a sociology of bodies because, few of us would disagree, our bodies matter like never before. We are an aging population and, as we age, attention is drawn to the failing and ailing body. (Although a runner—or perhaps because I'm a runner—my right quad hurts as I compose these lines.) We are an obese population, as everyone in the media seems to remind us. Our diets are larded with sugar and processed foods. We don't get enough exercise. We enroll in gyms and weight-loss programs, spending millions of dollars on our self-care, and then neglect our resolutions. And people, especially women, spend other dollars adorning their bodies and even re-sculpting them.

Why bodies have not been on the sociological radar screen bears discussion. Is it because we all have them—bodies? And we become accustomed to them, even as we know that our right leg hurts?! Or is it because many sociologists are preoccupied with quite dire predicaments of poverty, globalization, war, terror, cities, global warming, education, families, and the like? These are not mutually exclusive explanations. But there is a prior explanation, which returns us to the 17th century, when **the Enlightenment** liberated Europe from thousands of years of ignorance, blind habit, religious dogma, and strife. This led to a society with too many calories and not enough physical motion. Let's see how we got there, and what we might do about it.

Life 'before' Descartes

The body did not become an interesting topic, although it should have been, until only a few hundred years ago. For most of the Middle Ages, Catholicism viewed the body as dirty, a vehicle of sin. The Enlightenment or Age of Reason ended the Middle Ages, replacing religious dogma with scientific method. Science, cities, industry, paved roads and highways, medicine and health care, public education, railroads, air and space travel, and the Internet all emerged from the period, beginning about 1600, to which we give the name **modernity**. Only in modernity did bodies become a significant issue, although René Descartes got us thinking about bodies over 400 years ago.

What was human life like before the dawn of the 17th century? Until the **Industrial Revolution** of the 18th and 19th centuries, life for most Europeans and almost everyone outside of Europe, was more **pre-modern** than modern. They couldn't take survival for granted, let alone enjoy cable TV. Even today two-thirds of the world's seven billion people live in Third-World societies, such as those found in sub-Saharan Africa and parts of Asia and Latin America.

Almost everyone farmed, before which they were engaged in hunting and gathering. Later, we will examine a Mexican tribe still involved in chasing down their prey for food that will afford us insights into how to live healthier lives today. Also, almost everyone walked or ran; mechanical conveyances came on the scene late, when plotted on the long timeline of world history. The internal combustion engine powering automobiles is barely over 100 years old, stemming from the late 19th century when Karl Benz patented first a two-stroke and later a four-stroke engine for use in his cars.

Although people were hardier during the Middle Ages (from about 300 AD to 1600 AD), life was so difficult that the average life expectancy of people in the year 1400 was the mid-twenties. Bodies were succumbing right and left, from infant mortality, plague, warfare, civic crime, poor sanitation, limited public health, and medicine based on mystical notions of exorcism and leeching. The plagues of the mid-1300s killed off nearly a majority of Europeans, suggesting that there was real need for a rational perspective on bodies and health that did not emerge until the Enlightenment some 200 or 300 years later. The Black Death was spread by the humble rat. And medicine did not advance rapidly until the 20th century, when we cured polio and invented penicillin. The medical project of modernity is not complete; we are still unable to cure cancer or HIV.

Before bodies there was a book. A French philosopher named René Descartes (1956 [1637]), in *Discourse on Method*, suggested that the human being is actually both a mind and a body, splitting us into two components. Philosophers call this splitting an act of philosophical **dualism**. Descartes was not oblivious to the body. Rather, he was struggling to displace the heavy weight of the Catholic Church in Europe, which, he felt, kept intellectual creativity in check. Thus he asked himself a single foundational question: Of what can I be certain? For the millennium of the Middle Ages, the correct answer, for theologians St. Augustine and St. Aquinas, was the existence of God. But Descartes, although religious himself, offered a different perspective. He said that there is knowledge prior to our knowledge of God and that is self-knowledge—our certain knowledge that we are thinking beings who are doing the asking of these and other questions. "I think, therefore I am," Descartes wrote. Thinking came before running.

This small philosophical discovery led to one of the greatest revolutions the world has ever known. We call that intellectual revolution the Enlightenment, which elevated scientific method over faith. The Enlightenment ushered in **empiricism**, an approach to knowledge grounded not in the Bible but in the scientific method, which gathered knowledge from observation and experiment. From Descartes' insight stemmed the confidence to know and manipulate the world around us, the empirical world of sense experience. Descartes made Isaac Newton's physics possible, which led, eventually, to the Industrial Revolution. If nature could be known, it could be utilized for human purposes, in agriculture, medicine, industry, even, unfortunately, warfare.

From Ford's Factory to the Office Cubicle to 'Officing' at Starbucks

'Modernity' comprises the 17th century Enlightenment and the Industrial Revolution that began about 200 years later. The Enlightenment paved the way for industrialization, as Francis Bacon proclaimed that "knowledge is power." That also sounds like a self-help slogan! In effect, a sense of human efficacy leads to dominion over nature—conquering polio and harnessing water power and later the very atom for energy. By the early 20th century, Frederick Taylor (1998) developed **scientific management**. This approach sought to maximize factory productivity through social-scientific time-and-motion studies that would provide insights into how best to organize the workplace in order to get the most out of workers in their interactions with machines. And Taylor inspired Henry Ford, who helped put America on wheels using the assembly line to mass produce automobiles.

Europe and England emerged slowly from the agricultural economies and religious dogma of the Middle Ages. One can identify four stages of industrial development. All of these stages unfolded under **capitalism**, an economic system based on the personal right to hold wealth, start businesses, and turn a profit.

- 1700s–1900, slow industrial production with limited output; beginning of the manufacturing system and collective bargaining (unions); subsistence wages; factory workers lived in cities and many others lived in rural areas and farmed.
- 1900–World War II, **mass production** based on Ford's assembly line; wages rose and people shopped for more than meager necessities. National and international markets for goods emerged.
- 1950s–80s, bureaucratic capitalism, with a shift from factory to office work, the rise of **credentialism** and the need for an educated workforce; many could now satisfy not only their basic needs but also their 'wants,' aided by credit buying; peopled purchased their own homes, often in suburbia.
- 1990s–today, globally interconnected **laptop capitalism** with a flexible, educated workforce but also a vast service sector with wages barely above the subsistence level, the decline of unions, and specialized markets served by just-in-time production; now people shop 24/7, including online.

This fourth stage also involves the **de-industrialization** of the urban northeast, leading to vast migration to Texas, Florida, and California (see Bluestone and Harrison 1982). You may have purchased this book online. If you are consulting a bound copy of the book, it was printed 'just in time'—as soon as you ordered it. In this way, warehouses full of inventory (unsold units) disappear.

During the first phase of the Industrial Revolution, workers labored in factories, both small and large. At first, these workers had skills carried over from the artisanship of the Middle Ages, when they learned their crafts through oral traditions and apprenticeship. During the second phase, they continued to work in factories, but these were large factories governed by Henry Ford's social technology of mass production, with heavy use of machinery. Levels of skill fell from the early to later phase of industrialization, from artisan-like factory labor to the de-skilled labor of the assembly line. The second stage lasted from about 1900, the early years of Taylor and Ford, until some time after World War II when **blue-collar factory labor** was gradually replaced by **white-collar office work**. This third stage of industrialization (or post-industrialism, as some [Bell 1973] view it) involved a major dispersion of work from the factory to the office as industrial production was further mechanized and a greater portion of our economy involved the provision of services such as education, health care, and entertainment. During this stage, work, including factory work, was organized bureaucratically (with task specialization and a top-down chain of command). Also during this stage, which Max Weber suggests is coincident with the rise of the middle class, union membership declined as white-collar office workers viewed themselves as members of management.

Post-World War II white-collar workers were no longer housed in factories but in modernist high-rise office towers and in low-slung, suburban 'industrial parks.' These credentialed workers labor with head, not hand, although that is something of a misrepresentation because they write and type memos, certainly a kind of physical labor, and experience the confinement of the desk and office cubicle.

During the fourth stage, which can be dated from the advent of the Internet beginning in the late 1980s, many do not work in downtown towers, with physical segmentation (e.g., offices and elevators) and organizational hierarchy. Instead, with the aid of laptop computers and smart phones, they office 'anytime/anywhere,' untethered to the physical space of the office. Laptops and smart phones are the new factories, and emailing and texting the new labor process. The organization of work in this emerging era of **telecommuting** would seem to be more egalitarian, with workers functioning as independent contractors but also frequently not enjoying company benefits, union membership, and the collegiality of the workplace (Agger 2004; Dyer-Witheford 1999).

The era of mass production (or what Antonio Gramsci termed **Fordism**) makes available consumer goods, from clothes to cars, that have slender margins of profit; that is, their manufacturing cost is not much lower than their retail cost. Ford took the gamble that he would amass large profits, as low prices made possible by these slender profit margins would enable him to sell more cars, such as his Model Ts. A quickened production process could churn out hundreds of vehicles a day, compared with the slower, more painstaking process of making a Rolls Royce by hand. The Rolls had to be priced expensively because few 'units' were sold. Model Ts and later F-150s, by contrast, could be priced just above cost because many thousands would be affordable to workers, like Ford's own, in Detroit and eventually in a national market.

The **assembly-line system** enabled mass production. Originally, Ford's workers moved from station to station on the production line. There, they would perform specialized tasks such as securing tires to the chassis and installing windshields. They would not have to be trained to manufacture the whole automobile, but only to perform repetitive chores that could be readily mastered. Eventually, Ford recognized that the whole process could be quickened by automating the assembly line, bringing the car-under-assemblage to the workers, who would now perform only a single task while remaining physically in one spot.

This raises the question of whether this highly specialized assembly-line system 'alienates' workers, denying them feelings of creativity, originality, and mastery. The sociologist Max Weber, who was writing at the end of the 19th and beginning of the 20th centuries, viewed this sort of work as routine (**routinization** was his term for this) and not a source of personal satisfaction. Emile Durkheim, a contemporary of Weber, lamented the loss of community in this factory-like urban world, a condition he termed **anomie**, one of the most famous sociological concepts. And **alienation** was Karl Marx's term for work that is routine, anomic, and poorly paid, an outcome that he traced to the new capitalist order in which labor itself becomes a commodity, to be bought and sold. He felt that capitalism turns workers into commodities.

The more fragmented jobs were, the greater the division of labor, workers would need to be paid, given that their low-level skills, requiring little training or education, would be abundantly available in the labor market. It is open to debate whether automobiles of high quality can be assembled through a process that fragments labor and does not involve a sense of artisan-like craft and pride of production. In his book, *False Promises*, the sociologist Stanley Aronowitz (1992) recounts his own experience of working in an auto plant. He details the drudgery and alienation experienced by most workers.

Agribusiness and the Mass Production of Calories

Henry Ford's mass-production system, applied to farming and food, has liberated us from hunger and scarcity for people lucky enough to have jobs. Yet **body problems** in affluent but sedentary societies have actually increased in the meantime. This is partly because we work in office cubicles or in more flexible settings as we 'office' in our cars and homes and even at Starbucks. We drive everywhere and we work sitting down. The major occupational health hazards are carpal-tunnel syndrome and musculo-skeletal problems from repetitive word-processing and phone use performed with poor posture. And now food is so abundant that we can obtain it anytime/anywhere, just in time to satisfy our cravings. And the foods available are usually calorie-dense, salty, and fatty. Identifying how we can break out of this cycle is one of my book's challenges.

Fordism eventually led to **agribusiness**, farming on the basis of the heavy use of technology, fertilizer, and pesticide, and yielding massive crops. Much as Adam Smith's (2003 [1776]) **market capitalism** governed by an invisible hand evolved into oligopolies, cartels, and even monopolies as **capital** (productive wealth) became centralized after the Great Depression of the 1920s and 1930s, so American family farming evolved into corporate agriculture. This not only changed the ways that farmers lived and work; it greatly affected the food chains linking farms, slaughterhouses, supermarkets, restaurants, and school cafeterias. Agribusiness led to unprecedented production of inexpensive calories, in the surprising form of corn converted into **high-fructose corn syrup** and used as a starch (sugar), and in marbled meat from animals fed not on a free range but in pens, stuffed not with grass but with corn and other animal byproducts (Pollan 2006). As Upton Sinclair (2006) documented in his classic 1906 book *The Jungle*, slaughterhouses were early converts to the Fordist model of mass output, alienated working conditions and animal cruelty. Later, big farming and big meat converged in the phenomenon of themed restaurants, beginning with the Big Mac.

It is tempting to view body problems as outcomes of individual choices, such as eating too much (and the wrong things), not getting enough exercise, drinking too much alcohol and caffeine, generally not taking care of yourself. All these things may be true, but I prefer to look at these body problems as sociological outcomes of major shifts and trends in social structure. This is not an either/or: people make choices, but under the influence of advertising and peer pressure and in the absence of clear alternatives. I identify two trends as impacting individual consumer choices: the abundance of food (often delivered 'fast') that are laden with simple carbohydrates (e.g., sugar) instead of complex carbs (e.g., oatmeal), and the era of the automobile, which transports us to Jack in the Box and allows us to get around without exercising anything but our foot on the gas pedal.

Fast Food, Eisenhower, the McDonald Brothers

Eric Schlosser (2002) in *Fast Food Nation* chronicles the emergence of a fast-food diet (the so-called **standard American diet** or **SAD**) from the replacement of walking and physical labor by driving and office work and the unprecedented supply of largely empty calories. The rise of fast food can be directly linked to Eisenhower's interstate highway system of the 1950s and the purchase of the original McDonald brothers' San Bernardino, California drive-up hamburger restaurant by Ray Kroc, a World War I generation comrade in arms of the other great genius of **theming**, Walt Disney (Kay 1997).

At first, McDonald's hamburgers were merely efficient and inexpensive. The first McDonald's, before franchising by Kroc, was not a drive-in; patrons had to get out of their cars and walk in. Eventually, McDonald's became a symbol of a certain breezy and mobile **lifestyle**, much as Disneyland represented escape from a humdrum routine, a fantasy land of small-town neighborliness (on theming and American fantasy see Fjellman 1992; Gottdiener 2001; Spurlock 2005). George Ritzer (2004) has written of the **McDonaldization** of society, suggesting that fast, cheap, standardized food has become a metaphor for work and life in post-World War II America and now globally.

Cities, Suburbs, the End of Walking

Henry Ford and his auto-maker corporate colleagues decided to buy up urban trolley systems, requiring that people motor to work in private cars, first in cities and then from the bedroom communities called suburbs to their downtown work. The first American suburb, Levittown, was built on Long Island, NY in 1947, a reasonable symbolic beginning of a postmodern, post-urban era. In earlier societies it was assumed that people had to walk as well as do physical labor. They lived either in cities or in rural towns. Now, people can spend nearly their entire day sitting down, whether behind the wheel of a mass-produced vehicle, at the desk, or around the dinner table of a cookie-cutter suburban house.

What nutritionists call the **French quandary** describes the odd fact that the French do not stint on butter and calories, and drink plenty of wine, but generally do not have weight problems, at least by comparison to Americans. For the most part the French do not 'work out'—think of gyms with elliptical trainers and treadmills on which people do the hard labor of exercise. The French quandary is explained in part by the fact that the French walk a lot and are on their feet. It is difficult to drive and park in Paris and so Parisians expend calories by walking. This is not a calculated health strategy but a pre-modern habit carried forward. Urban walking in Europe is sited in delightful medieval cities with manageable dimensions. As well, the French are served and serve themselves smaller portions than Americans are accustomed to, limiting their access to calories.

DISCUSSION QUESTIONS

1. Henry Ford was not a philosopher, and yet his innovations in mass production profoundly changed the modern world in which we live. What are the costs and benefits of his innovations?
2. During the Middle Ages, life was hard and people died early. Were there any advantages to life in the Middle Ages?
3. Why do people like standardized products provided by chains such as restaurants and hotels?

II: Too Much of a Good Thing, and The Invention of Exercise

﹌﹌✕﹌﹌

We all tend to experience historical amnesia; we forget the past. Or perhaps we never knew it. When I was a college student and I learned that the category of childhood was nearly non-existent during the Middle Ages, I was really surprised (see Shorter 1975). Children were viewed as miniature adults, of whom farm and then factory work was expected. We didn't carve out a special category for needy, adorable children until the 19th century Victorian era, as we tried to convince women and children to leave the labor force to men. We thus created the whole realm of **domesticity**, including childhood within it.

By the same token, 'exercise' is an even newer invention. When we began to drive to work in office buildings, and created available and inexpensive, fatty and sugar-laden fast food, we noticed that people's waistlines began swelling. And we also realized that cardio-vascular illness was increasing rapidly. And so exercise was what people do in that compartment of their lives reserved for working out—another type of work, to be sure. Doctors realized that people need to sweat and breathe deeply, especially if they don't get that in their jobs.

Perfect Storm: Money, Sedentary Jobs, Cars, Calories

The more than 2,000 years of human history before World War II could be called the phase of hunger (or **caloric deficit**). Life was an unending struggle to match the expenditure of calories in farming and early industrial work with sufficient calories from food. Industrialization during the 18th and 19th centuries ushered in a phase of **caloric equilibrium**, with the beginning of large-scale agriculture and food production matched by a combination of agricultural and factory labor that involved relatively heavy physical toil. This equilibrium might have described life for Henry Ford's own employees during the 1920s. Finally, we have entered a phase of **caloric surplus**, with the end of rural life and agriculture for most in affluent countries, the shift from heavy to light industry, office work and telecommuting, and the advent of the automobile and now the Internet.

When I say "we," I omit those among us (10 percent or more of our people) and in Third-World societies who endlessly struggle to get enough calories to survive.

Some of the Third World live in villages and in the countryside, while others (think of the Indian city of Bombay [Mumbai], one of the world's largest) inhabit urban slums. To portray 'the end of hunger' applies, at most, to people in affluent Western European, North American, and some Pacific Rim nations, with a smattering of city dwellers in advanced South American countries such as Argentina. But even these nations have significant strata of poor people, with perhaps Scandinavia the only exception.

This era has brought a perfect storm of body problems—obesity, high-blood pressure, heart disease, osteoporosis, and depression linked to the lack of physical activity. Yes, we *can* have too many abundant and available calories, especially where we don't expend these as fuel in work or leisure. Our historic conceptions of the 'good life' have stressed freedom from hunger, a laudable goal, but have not anticipated caloric abundance coupled with sedentary lifestyles. Indeed, most 17th century, age-of-reason considerations of a good society, a utopia, stressed political freedom, the end of religious dogma, and the elimination of hunger. Think of the Thanksgiving cornucopia and its image of abundance. Bodies were not considered, except inasmuch as the emaciated body of the pre-modern era was to be replaced by the satiated body of 'the consumer.' And the consumer was to be 'sovereign,' in charge of his or her own decisions. Never was it considered that the sovereign consumer would be a couch-bound glutton.

It was assumed that enlightened people would make rational choices about what they put into their bodies. The rise of capitalist economic theory during the 18th century left consumption unexamined. The consumer, the rational chooser, was not susceptible to advertising because, in the mid-18th century, the fundamental human challenge was simply to consume enough calories to survive. Fast food was not yet on the menu (see Ewen 1976; Leiss 1976).

In that light, the end of hunger would seem to bring uncompromised benefits. And yet many people are awash in too many calories, tempted (and able) to overeat, and thus running new health risks. The risk of starvation and inadequate nutrition has been replaced by the risk of overindulgence in calories and fat. Although it is not natural for people to overeat, the tendency to gorge may be hard-wired into our survival instincts as people in pre-industrial societies swung from famine to fast to famine, depending on the success of their hunting and on the seasonality of crops. But even when feasting, putting on the pounds in anticipation of lean times ahead, early people burned off their calories in work, including hunting and farming. Today, these calories are stored and converted into fat because manual work has been largely replaced by sedentary work and inactive lifestyles. And so the abundance of calories is matched by an end to physical labor—to exercise, by another name—bringing with it all sorts of negative health consequences. We are a sedentary society that also overeats. But we are still also an anxious society. We are stressed because our jobs are not secure, we spend beyond our means, and we sense that we are unhealthy. Instead of addressing causes of this stress, we medicate it, as we discuss later.

We are tempted by calorie-dense foods such as chocolate and bacon that taste better than apples and oatmeal, unless we retrain ourselves to like the leaner foods! We are predisposed to want foods that will prevent us from starving. As well, food surrounds us in ways that it did not even as recently as a generation ago. When I grew up in the 1950s and 1960s, eating was done at home or in restaurants. There were vending machines, but these were not found everywhere. Although many of us were middle-class, food was not available around every corner. Today, one cannot drive down the street without passing a fast-food restaurant or a gas station that doubles as a restaurant and grocery store. Work places and schools offer relatively inexpensive and convenient fast food. Temptation abounds, and many of us have the money to satisfy temptation. When the first McDonald's opened in my town during my last year of high school in 1969, none of us would have expected 'McDonaldization,' a world dominated by themed throw-away products, including processed food.

The Distressed Heart

Those who in the 1600s imagined a better world, a modern one, based on freedom from hunger and on political liberty, could not have imagined our postmodern (or perhaps 'plusmodern') predicament: too much 'modernity'—calories, sitting, automobiles—can actually harm us. Given the physical struggle to survive, cardio-vascular disease would not have seemed a likely outcome of the better world people sought. Even the meat people ate then was lean and grass-fed, not the marbled, fatty kind raised by the mass-production livestock industry.

This is a curious relationship: the engine of modernity, Ford's mass production system, frees us from starvation when applied to agriculture and meatpacking and yet it creates new health problems, including too many unexpended calories. In our rush to escape war, disease, high infant mortality, above all hunger—we shed the very mind–body connection that ensured that people, in living their daily lives, would stress their hearts and expend energy. Perhaps we need to look backward as well as forward in imagining a world in which the mind and body are connected in activities ('exercise,' or maybe we need a better word) that burn calories, stimulate the cardio-vascular system, and give us the glow of fulfillment derived from a spell at the gym or on the roads.

The **New Left** and feminist politics of the sixties, stressing the unity of mind and body, led to an exercise movement in the 1970s that viewed exercise as beneficial for heart health and weight control and also framed exercise as a valid leisure activity in its own right. Running, cycling, swimming, hiking, and walking were seen to provide meaning to people otherwise stuck in boring and office-bound employment.

Kenneth Cooper and Aerobics

History proceeds according to no master plan. It is "cunning," to use the philosopher Hegel's phrase. A doctor in Dallas, Texas and a track coach at the University of Oregon played major roles in reorienting Americans' thinking about body politics, beginning in the 1960s and 1970s. An even more obscure track coach and exercise theorist in faraway New Zealand gave the Oregon coach insights that would change America.

That these pioneers of **aerobics** (Kenneth Cooper), **jogging** (Bill Bowerman), and marathoning (Arthur Lydiard) caught on and created a revolution in regular Americans' lives is partly explained by the combined effects of caloric surpluses, driving, sedentary work and the 1960s attention to personal life and bodies. Affluence may have given us the Golden Arches and desk jobs that do not burn through calories; affluence also gave many people more leisure time. They used this time to find their bliss athletically, a revolutionary development in human history. Although earlier societies had room for sports, often reserved for elites, now whole nations of middle-class people, from New Zealand to the United States, are becoming weekend warriors and even daily warriors.

They are doing so to get fit and stay healthy. Some get hooked and stay with it even after they lost a few belt sizes. We cannot tell this story of ordinary people trying to solve their body problems without considering Cooper's (1968) 'aerobics,' first popularized in his book of the same title. Aerobics was not poetry but a science of cardiovascular exertion and oxygen consumption.

Cooper argued that one could achieve heart health by consuming ample quantities of oxygen through exercise. This exercise could be taken three or four times a week, in no more than half-hour stints. This level of exercise (running, biking, swimming, even walking) would be 'aerobic'—that is, it would utilize oxygen. But it wouldn't be so taxing that people would go into 'oxygen debt' or deficit, that extreme feeling one has while sprinting and gasping for air. Aerobic exercise could be done while talking; indeed, the talk test (whether one can carry on a conversation during the activity) became a nearly universal guideline for this gentle but exerting activity.

The heart and lungs would benefit greatly from this regular and gentle exercise, according to Cooper. Many Americans embarked on fitness using Cooper's well-thumbed book as a guide. Cooper viewed exercise as sweaty and perhaps depriving, and he made no bones about how this routine required self-sacrifice, especially at the beginning as people got off the couch and laced up their running shoes. However, Cooper also made the point that anyone can do this; one does not have to be an elite, Olympic-bound athlete. The pace of one's efforts has only to be sufficient to derive the **training effect**, a heart-rate level sufficient to stress the heart gently. This cardiac stress was a good thing for Cooper, and it derives from the Canadian Hans Selye's (1956, 1974) earlier writings on how physical stress produces healthy adaptations as people's bodies learn to cope with gradually increasing loads. The heart, as a muscle, needs stress, but only stress when it is produced by activities such as running and cycling that require one to gulp down large quantities of oxygen. A scary movie won't suffice to raise one's heart rate!

Lydiard, Bowerman, and Jogging

During the 1960s, I grew up in Eugene, Oregon, and I remember that, all of a sudden it seemed, average citizens were jogging around the streets. Bill Bowerman, the University of Oregon track coach who would become a founder of Nike as well as a coaching legend, had gone to New Zealand with his track team and brought back the radical new ideas of Arthur Lydiard. Lydiard gave Bowerman the 'jogging' idea, a way for regular people, not only star athletes, to keep fit. Lydiard trained himself and then turned to training Olympic, gold-medal winning athletes such as Peter Snell. His book *Running the Lydiard Way* (Lydiard 1978) explains his basic principles.

There are several important themes in Lydiard. First, he wanted to train speedy milers the same way he would train marathoners. Most of their running would be long and slow (a relative term, admittedly!). They would pile up the miles, run at a conversational pace, and thus develop full aerobic capacity. In plain English, they would become highly efficient running machines. They would then fine-tune their capabilities by running fast for a few weeks before their chosen events. This faster running, often called **intervals**, would sharpen them by teaching them to run fast in an **anaerobic** (oxygen-debt) **state**. Lydiard believed that anaerobic fitness would be maximized when overlaid onto a base of long, slow miles. He thus trained Snell and his other prodigies to run marathons, even though Snell would eventually medal at the 800- and 1500-meter distances in the 1960 and 1964 Olympics.

Another Lydiard contribution was the notion of **periodization**, meaning that the runner could not be at his or her peak indefinitely. They could peak only once or a few times a year, those periods when they would sharpen with **speed work** after having amassed a large base of aerobic (conversational) miles. These ideas, taken together, gave Bowerman the idea that there had to be periodization within the runner's weeks of training. A hard and difficult effort one day must be followed by a day or two of easier running in order to allow the athlete to recover from and adapt to the self-imposed stress of the harder workout.

Lydiard taught Bowerman that many well-conditioned athletes, and almost all regular couch-potato citizens, are undertrained. They are far from achieving their full aerobic capacity. Hence, he prescribed 100-mile weeks of running for his athletes and even for weekend warriors intending to run a marathon. Out of shape when he first traveled to New Zealand, Bowerman joined Lydiard on his daily runs and quickly regained the fitness he enjoyed as a college athlete.

These ideas and experiences convinced Bowerman that he could train his own Oregon athletes better and indeed bring this gentle form of aerobic running to the citizens of Eugene. He wrote a book about 'jogging,' a new word to describe gentle long-distance running performed at a conversational pace (Bowerman and Harris 1967).

Along with Cooper's work on aerobics, Bowerman's recommendation of jogging for all Americans paved the way for the **first running revolution**, which occurred during the 1970s. Suddenly, it seemed, millions of Americans were running and pursuing fitness. They were entering 10K races and even marathons. An additional stimulus of this first running revolution was the televised heroics of Florida-based runner Frank Shorter, a Yale graduate and future lawyer, at the tragedy-stained Munich Olympics in 1972. Although Shorter was already well-known in the elite marathon community, having won the prestigious Japanese marathon at Fukuoka four times, his victory in the Olympic marathon surprised and energized Americans who watched him enter the Olympic stadium on television. Shorter gave a face to running in the United States, and we quickly learned that he was witty and intelligent. He was also skinny and seemingly unathletic, giving hope to non-football-playing people that they could succeed in running and other aerobic sports.

Cooper, Bowerman (through Lydiard), and Shorter inspired Americans to hit the roads, but not in the way that Henry Ford did. Initially, running was for fitness and people tallied their aerobic points (Cooper's measuring stick) and their running miles. Gradually, running came to be viewed as recreation, escape, personal fulfill- ment. Some people were running away, others toward—what? According to George Sheehan, who they were meant to be. Magazines such as *Runner's World* became cult-like as regular people became 'athletes'—people who work out regularly and view themselves as such. You didn't need to be Frank Shorter in order to finish first in the great race of life!

Growing up in Eugene, I remember not only people jogging in the neighborhoods, but also Bowerman's powerful University of Oregon track teams as they competed for and won the NCAA championship. I made the connection: watching Dyrol Burleson run 3:58.6, the first sub-four-minute mile ever run at Hayward Field, as the stands rocked, was tied to the new jogging phenomenon.

We could all become athletes, an insight I gained from my life in Eugene that car- ried forward into my own running career. A book about Bowerman (*Bowerman and the Men of Oregon* by Kenny Moore [2006]) situates his theories about running and his coaching endeavors in my hometown. His team ran up a hill by my house, clad in long johns dyed emerald green, imprinting on me the importance of doing hard and regular physical work. This was the same hill on which Steve Prefontaine, the phenomenal, front-running, Oregon middle-distance expert, lost his life in a 1975 car accident.

Figure 2.1 Burleson outrunning Cunliffe in 3:58:6.
Source: Used with permission of University of Oregon digital collections.

Bowerman liked to tinker with running shoe designs in order to make his athletes faster. From his work room emerged the famous waffle trainer that helped launch the Nike Company, originally called Blue Ribbon Sports. The waffle trainer was released in 1974, following the classic Cortez running shoe first produced in 1966. Bowerman wanted Nike to be a people's company providing shoes for the everyday jogger as well as the elite miler. Little could he have imagined how Nike would become a global and branded entity. I purchased my first waffles in 1976, the year I started running.

The empowering of amateur, everyday athletes like Bowerman's citizens responded to changes in society such as sedentary lifestyles, office work, poor diet paradoxically including too many calories, obesity. It also responded to 'alienation'—the sense that one's life, work especially, lacks intrinsic meaning. For non-runners and non-athletes, running around in circles through neighborhoods before the crack of dawn might seem even less meaningful! As with all things social and human, this depends on one's perspective. It is not that running is an elevated activity but that pursuing a discipline such as daily running builds character and also provides physical and emotional benefits that are quite addictive.

Figure 2.2 Bowerman mentors Prefontaine.
Source: Used with permission of University of Oregon digital collections.

DISCUSSION QUESTIONS

1. Henry Ford's workers got a lot of exercise in manual labor, even as the innovation of mass production led to a surplus of inexpensive calories. How did subsequent changes in work combine with mass-produced calories to lead, quite suddenly, to an overweight America?
2. Do you think that the jogging and aerobic revolution of the 1960s and 1970s stemmed from people's dissatisfaction with their sedentary lifestyles, or did it have different causes?

III: Body Sciences

In a society prone to quantify and measure things, it is no surprise that we would defer to **body sciences**, of which the most prominent is medicine. Medical science improves on folk wisdom passed along orally, which helped people address their health problems for over a thousand years before the Enlightenment. Folk wisdom can be helpful, such as your grandmother's recipe for chicken soup, to be imbibed when you catch a cold. But it has its limitations. It won't necessarily help you deal effectively with high blood pressure or the need for a hip replacement. One might respond that most people in agricultural societies did not experience high blood pressure because they got exercise in their daily lives, weren't obese, and did not have diets high in refined sugar. Rural poverty had an upside, as long as one could eke out enough calories to survive.

And so my critique of the **medical model** of the body, which I unfold in this chapter, does not turn back the clock before the Salk polio vaccine and MRI scans. I prefer to live today, as long as we also recognize the limitations of the medical model. Body sciences do not by themselves solve body problems, especially where we measure the wrong things.

Medicalizing the Body

Taylor's scientific management of labor emerged from the general optimism of the 17th and 18th centuries that nature can be controlled using positive sciences. **Positivism** is a theory of knowledge that attempts to be perfectly objective about the world, standing outside of time and space as one utilizes mathematical methods of great precision. This positive knowledge is best expressed in laws of cause and effect, such as the 1980s discovery that a retrovirus originally acquired from an African chimp causes HIV, which in turn causes AIDS.

Positivism was transported from the natural sciences to the social sciences by Auguste Comte, the father of sociology, during the 19th century. He modeled his new discipline on the physics of Newton, who in his laws of motion captured the cause-and-effect mathematical positivism that proved intoxicating to Europeans awakening from the slumber of the Middle Ages. Sociology was to be social physics, according to Comte, outlining general laws of modern progress. Sociology would be a trouble-shooting discipline that would help industrial Europe make on-course corrections as social problems, viewed as temporary episodes, disrupted progress. For the early sociologists, including the Chicago School, these problems were often urban as people in cities coped with crowding, crime, unemployment, pollution, and the influx of freed slaves from the south and immigrants from Europe and Ireland.

This view of social problems dominated U.S. sociology from the late 1930s to the 1960s (see Talcott Parsons [1951] and Robert Merton [1957]). During the tumult of the sixties, scholars and students began to challenge the views that sociology could be completely objective, using mathematical methods, and that society was more or less peacefully moving forward, toward capitalism, the male-run nuclear family, the militarized nation state, and a world system dominated by Western countries. Parsons' functionalism was challenged by a radical and critical sociology (Gouldner 1970; Mills 1959; O'Neill 1972) that drew from various European thinkers such as Karl Marx and the **Frankfurt School**. Critics of Parsons conceptualized social problems (the very subject of this book series) not as episodes to be healed with mere band-aids but as deep structural features such as racism, sexism, and poverty that require large-scale societal changes, even revolutions.

What I am calling 'body problems' in this book can be viewed either as minor irruptions, viruses almost, that can be eased with a dose of sociological medical science, or they can be viewed, as I prefer, as symptomatic outcomes of a society grounded in Cartesian dualism, alienated labor, and a corporate food supply. Both are valid frameworks, and both draw attention to important issues. Perhaps the band-aid approach focuses on solvable local issues, whereas the systemic approach concentrates on more global issues. The local and global blend in what some environmentalists now call the **glocal**, a perspective that sacrifices neither fine-grained detail nor the big picture.

The view that body problems are best addressed through positivist body sciences of the kind I will discuss in the rest of this chapter leads to **body industries**, treated in Chapter 4, such as gyms, weight-loss regimens, and even plastic surgery. This is very much an influence of the Enlightenment, which relied on Newton's physics to analyze problems in nature using quantitative methodologies and then deployed engineering to solve them. We have done the same thing with both labor and food, as I noted above. Now we do that with bodies, using medical science and its allied science of **nutritionism**.

We 'medicalize' the body by reducing its well-being to measurable characteristics such as weight, blood pressure, and cholesterol. If we are fitness-oriented, we might also use a stopwatch to measure the length of time it takes to run a mile (Dr. Cooper did that) or we might calculate the percentage of body fat and oxygen-uptake capacity (how much oxygen we can process). Indeed, many exercise physiologists believe that **oxygen uptake** (calculated as **VO_2 Max**) is a useful measure of overall fitness, even though measuring it requires an elaborate apparatus including a treadmill and breathing equipment. There are also measures of prostate health (for men) and of cervical health (for women).

It is now becoming clear that VO$_2$ Max does not perfectly predict performance; **running economy** may be more important—how well one uses oxygen. The two are linked: record setters have superb capacity for processing oxygen and they move efficiently, making the most of what they have. And, all things being equal, skinny people are the most efficient runners. Watching any race reveals that the winner is small and, as people stream in behind, their body shapes gradually expand until they look like the rest of us! This is running economy in action.

Beyond The Medical Model

One of the great achievements of the Enlightenment was the shift from dogma to science. It is now acceptable to look for answers to questions about the world in the world itself, through science, and not in certain sacred texts whose authority must not be questioned. Scientific method was to solve human problems via the social engineering of public policy.

By the 20th century, this gave us mass production, which we now use to produce not only automobiles but food. This has caused what I call body problems, which we try to resolve with mass-market body industries such as diets and gyms. Sometimes, those work, but more often they do not. They tend to fail because we embrace a medical model from the Enlightenment.

The medical model (Laing 1967) is a view of body problems grounded in the notions that the person is a body, separated from the mind, emotions, and will, the body can be studied scientifically, and medical professionals can prescribe cures for body problems. This model has saved millions of lives, extended life expectancy, and improved the quality of life for many. However, it has oversimplified body problems because it is grounded in Descartes' original splitting of the mind and body, what earlier I called 'dualism.' R. D. Laing first identified the medical model used in psychiatry to treat mental illness. He had doubts that this model gets to the heart of psychological distress, relying, as it does, on the assumption that problems of the self can be addressed in the same way as body problems. This early-sixties critique of psychiatry is foundational for later work in the critical sociology of health, illness, diet, and exercise, to which this book is a contribution.

This model neglects the idea that people are in fact unities of body and mind and that they can act with **agency**—a philosophical term for free will. They can take control of their lives and change the everyday ways they work, eat, exercise, dress themselves, travel. They can change their lifestyles, which, even the medical model recognizes, has a great deal of impact on health outcomes and risks. The medical model turns the person into a patient, defends the doctor's authority over the patient, and solves problems with prescriptions—of pills, weight loss, and further dependence on service providers.

One of the key features of the medical model is dependence on professionals who evaluate external indicators of our well-being, such as weight or cholesterol. To solve body problems, we visit doctors, physical therapists, masseurs and masseuses, nutritionists, personal trainers, aerobics-class leaders, hairdressers, manicurists, fashion consultants. There is nothing inherently wrong with **professionalism**; I want my physician to have earned medical degrees from legitimate universities and to have experience in the field. But professionalism, of which the medical model is a powerful example, renders the consumer/patient dependent on an authoritative expert, diminishing his or her ability to act in a problem-solving and preemptive way.

The medicalized body is passive and consumes pills and services dispensed by professionals. The de-medicalized body seeks professional care only when necessary, as a last resort. Calloused runners, for example, have experienced so much wear and tear that they become experts at self-diagnosis. They read the sports-medicine literature on running injuries; they talk to other runners; they surf the Web; they occasionally visit doctors. They learn to 'listen to their bodies,' a term that applies equally to monitoring one's breathing and effort during a race as to monitoring one's overall level of fitness and health.

Just as the medical model would solve body problems with prescriptions of this and that, so it underemphasizes the role of psychosomatic processes such as optimism, will, desire, or their absence. This is not to say that a pulled muscle is simply in one's head but to notice that the power of positive thinking is immense, both in producing effort and in recovery. A popular term is 'empowering,' the exercise of will power. An empowered person takes charge of his or her body problems, de-medicalizing them and perhaps even de-problematizing them. That is, you can find your own solutions, stretching out the pulled muscle without a trip to the doctor; and you can decide that your lack of energy in the morning simply reflects that you have been idle too long and need to learn some new habits, such as morning exercise (and then eating breakfast).

Martin Seligman (2002) argues that psychologists need to focus on the happy person, not only the unhappy one (see http://www.authentichappiness.sas.upenn.edu/Default.aspx). The positive-psychology movement he helped initiate agrees with Norman Vincent Peale (1996), a father of the self-help movement, that one's attitude helps determine whether one is successful or not in one's chosen tasks.

The Annual Physical

The American Medical Association advises Americans to know their risk factors (e.g., whether they smoke or have a parent who had cancer) and to live a healthy lifestyle. American health care professionals recommend an annual physical exam in which the 'medical' body is assessed. Women are advised to have periodic breast-cancer screenings after the age of 40, and both sexes are urged to have colonoscopies beginning at age 50 (unless there is a family history of colon cancer, in which case these screenings begin earlier). No one with health insurance or independent financial means should ignore these visits inasmuch as they help us protect ourselves defensively through regimes of diet, exercise, and medication.

The annual physical is at the core of medicalized body problems. If blood pressure is too high, blood-pressure medication can be prescribed. But what about the rest of the year? Certainly, lifestyle insights may emerge from the annual physical: use less salt; cut down on caffeine and alcohol; get exercise. But, for the most part, the busy physician is not going to play the role of counselor as well as healer. The 'whole' person will not be considered, but only his or her vital statistics—the quantitative indicators of health, defined as the absence of illness. But what of **wellness**, which includes mental health?

Most physicians, by training and via our culture, are Cartesians; they separate mind and body. To be sure, psychosomatic factors may play a role in illness. Too much anxiety takes a physical toll. Indeed, a huge drug industry has grown up around anxiety, stress, depression. This does not yield itself to quantitative indicators but rather to personal accounts, to the narratives patients, especially women, tell doctors as they recount their dissatisfaction with their own lives.

And so one leaves the physical exam, which may have a psychological component especially for women who report anxiety and depression, with a variety of prescriptions for problems of blood pressure, cholesterol, or depression. Big 'pharma' joins the other Fordist industries such as big food in seeking to make consumers dependent on their expensive wares. The estimated sales of blood-pressure medications is over $10 billion a year. What are problems of living, involving eating, exercise, and stress, are addressed pharmaceutically. While this can obviously be defended, the medical model of body problems tends to de-emphasize the mind–body unity by, in effect, treating the body as belonging to the realm of nature. Medical science is an arm of natural science, which, until Einstein's revolution in relativity, proceeds according to positivist procedures, aiming at pure objectivity.

But medical science falls short where it neglects the active mind–body, the person by another name, who bears responsibility for his or her own life. Bearing responsibility means that people can, through deliberate changes, alter the ways they use their bodies and minds, freeing themselves from a dependence on dosing doctors who see them only once a year for monitoring. While monitoring is necessary (checking blood levels of prescribed medications, for example), the whole person is on his or her own for the other 364 days of the year, time that matters to the overall well-being of the person.

By stressing illness and not wellness, the medical model of body problems chooses the same path as those who would solve social problems with band-aids. Sometimes, total change is necessary, as we see dramatically on reality TV shows that screen massive weight loss achieved not with surgery but through changes in eating, exercising, and living. The medical model could conceivably recommend these changes, perhaps prescribing a stint in a diet clinic for a morbidly obese patient. However, typically, the medical model would result in a combination of drugs for blood pressure and cholesterol and a **crash diet** designed to achieve, at least temporarily, a satisfactory **body mass index (BMI)**. As I discuss below, the BMI is imposed by medical and dietary professionals on a public willing to swallow whole the medical model that reduces health to a number.

The Invention of Obesity and the BMI

When I was a child, doctors monitored weight. Today, doctors use a somewhat more sophisticated, two-variable model, now also including height. A six-foot person can afford to weigh more than a person a foot shorter. The BMI establishes weight/height ideals for a public convinced that Americans are obese. Many annual physicals now include not only a weigh-in but the doctor's calculation of the patient's BMI, followed by a brief discussion of whether the person's number falls within the normal range or suggests obesity (rarely, insufficient weight). Because BMI is thought to be a more comprehensive number than weight alone, it has become the basis of a new demonology of obesity among physicians, dieticians, nutritionists, and even physical therapists.

Is America fat and getting fatter? A quick trip around the country, perhaps focusing on airports and malls, would certainly yield ample evidence to suggest that obesity is prevalent. And it is equally easy to connect obesity to serious health problems such as heart disease, **hypertension** (high blood pressure), and high cholesterol. Obesity could also be linked to anxiety and depression. And if one extended one's trip to include schools, one would find an alarming number of apparently overweight children and teenagers.

Oliver's (2006) *Fat Politics* challenges the notion that Americans are obese (but see Popkin [2009] for a counterargument). This is counter-intuitive, that is, it violates commonsense. Surely Oliver does not mean that Americans are lean and fit! He admits that when he began his study, he assumed, as most of us do, that Americans are dangerously obese and that this represents a relatively recent change. But he finds that how we measure and interpret weight influences our findings. He pays special attention to the thresholds, such as with the BMI, between normal weight and overweight. He finds the BMI to be quite imperfect, reflecting 1940s Met Life data suggesting a correlation between weight and life expectancy. He points out that there is no available medical science supporting the BMI's cut-points between normal weight and obesity. There is no hard evidence supporting the contention that being overweight by the BMI's standard is a health risk. In other words, the BMI as Oliver explains, reinforces our cultural penchant for thinness above all else.

Oliver concedes that there are correlations between obesity and health deficits and risks, but he concludes that obesity is not clearly the cause of these deficits. For example, people who are obese tend to have high blood pressure. And obese people may be more prone to high cholesterol. The blood pressure and cholesterol can kill you, but in and of themselves a few extra pounds may not be risky.

Indeed, the BMI, purporting to be an improvement over the old weight charts with which I was familiar as a kid, neglects to measure 'muscularity,' or, conversely, percentage of body fat. This is important because a unit of muscle weighs more than a unit of fat. All things being equal, people who lift weights and do other kinds of resistance training weigh *more* than do non-lifters. Few would disagree that lifting weights contributes to good health, both by burning calories directly and by strengthening the musculo-skeletal system in ways that can ward off brittle bones, a potential problem for aging women in particular.

And so certain famous athletes, especially black ones, are officially classified as overweight according to the BMI. These include Michael Jordan, Emmitt Smith, and Serena Williams! Michael Jordan, at the height of his career, was sinewy, strong, 'cut.' He was so lean that his muscularity raised his overall weight, leading to the erroneous conclusion that he exceeded the BMI norm for someone of his height. In other words, athletes, including weekend warriors, are *likely* to be overweight by BMI standards simply because they become more muscular than couch potatoes. And no exercise physiologist would deny that working out, both lifting and doing cardio work, has tremendous health benefits that are quite independent of one's weight.

While cardio work such as running, cycling, and using the elliptical trainer burns calories, it replaces fat with muscle, perhaps canceling the weight-reducing effect of raising the metabolism and burning calories. A better measure of health and fitness than the BMI is one's **resting heart rate**, which varies inversely with one's level of cardiac fitness. The fitter one is, the lower will be his or her resting heart rate. Now here is a single number that makes sense, and yet it is rarely considered at the annual physical. Whereas the average man has a resting heart rate of about 72, elite endurance athletes such as cyclist Lance Armstrong and the former tennis player Bjorn Borg had heart rates in the high 30s. Serious but non-professional amateur runners frequently have resting heart rates in the high 40s and low 50s. Recently, mine was 42, and I was at the time running 45 miles a week. Mileage-wise, I'm down in the 30s now and enjoying it more. (Professional marathoners frequently run 140 miles a week, which they accomplish with two-a-days!)

One reason we fixate on obesity is because weight previously, and now BMI, is a single easy number. But so is resting heart rate, which I contend is a better measure of fitness. Another reason is that we are vain, even narcissistic. We care more about how we look than what is 'inside,' including our good human qualities and our cardio-vascular health. Those Lipitor advertisements demystify this as they portray good-looking and apparently fit people engaged in active recreation who, in fact, have dangerously high cholesterol levels. The ad says, in effect, it is not enough to exercise and eat right; you should also take Lipitor to bring down your cholesterol, if it is too high. The marketing campaign is successful because the people in the ads appear healthy, fit, and even attractive on the outside, making us rethink the possible disconnect between 'inside' and 'outside.'

None of us wants to look obese, or be obese. The health risks are substantial, although, as I am arguing, it is not obesity per se that is the main risk but rather the lifestyle that caused obesity, probably including too little exercise and too many fatty foods. **Morbid obesity** (very overweight) may make it difficult and even impossible to live a healthy life, but simply being overweight with respect to the BMI categories is not only not necessarily a health risk but may be a health benefit *if* the extra pounds are a result of muscle and not fat.

People can be too thin, and some women, especially young women, are. **Eating disorders** abound in a culture that prizes girl-like figures, a sheer impossibility for most women. Women respond to the cultural norm of thinness by starving themselves (**anorexia**), binging and purging (**bulimia**), or engaging in **binge eating**. They weigh themselves constantly and keep food journals. Frequently, anorexics subsist on a meager 800 calories a day, an intake of fuel that makes exercise impossible (see http://www.pro-ana-nation.com).

Nutritionism

Just as it appears obvious that being overweight is a health risk, few doubt that people should take in the right amount and balance of necessary nutrients. However, we have just seen that what it means to be overweight is a tricky question, especially in the absence of medical science supporting the popular BMI scale. It is equally tricky to evaluate the claims by nutritionists that we should enhance our diet with certain nutrients, as **supplements**, if they are missing from our daily food—for example, a pill for vitamin C or B-complex.

Nutritionism breaks down our dietary needs into chemical and vitamin components. A great deal of medical research supports these efforts, even if there is lingering dispute over such issues as whether mega-doses of vitamin C ward off colds. However, Michael Pollan (2008) points out in his books on food theory that vitamin D and iron deficiencies cannot necessarily be remedied with supplements. There may be something about eating 'whole foods' that is magical for nutrition. Yes, Whole Foods is also an expensive organic-and-health-food chain that long ago betrayed (or perhaps creatively transformed) its hippie origins in Austin, Texas.

Instead we must eat in pre-modern ways, shunning processed, prepared, and packaged foods in favor of fresh, locally-grown food. Diets high in locally-grown vegetables are especially recommended by Pollan, not because he is a nutritionist but because he observes that so-called primitive cultures ate healthy food, as our new friends from Mexico, the Tarahumara do. The main challenge for early cultures was getting enough calories, not the right combinations of calories. For example, South American villagers might eat bread prepared from maize (corn), such as tortillas, various vegetables that they foraged, and beans for protein. This humble but healthy diet has global variations, for example in China, where rice might be substituted for maize. In such cultures, the rates of heart disease, high cholesterol, and high blood pressure are very low, probably because people eat whole and healthy food and also because they are highly ambulatory and engaged in physical work. Petrini's (2003) manifesto, *Slow Food*, argues for local cuisine consumed in convivial companionship, linking healthy diet with the social rewards of community. He wants to slow down not only eating but all of modern life, echoing themes I raise in my books *Fast Capitalism* (Agger 1989) and the sequel *Speeding Up Fast Capitalism* (Agger 2004).

Here we are introducing a distinction between **dieting** and **diet**, a distinction that becomes critical when we examine weight-loss programs. Diet*ing* is frequently designed to shed pounds, whereas diet is what we eat day in and day out. It is now generally agreed that crash diets don't work because they starve the person, who loses water weight, and then gorges because she craves what she is missing. The metabolism slows as we instinctively protect the body against starvation, and even weight loss slows. We really need to speed up the metabolism, achieved by exercise. (That can also be achieved by caffeine and diet pills, but those don't produce aerobic benefits.) What needs to change is our daily diet, usually larded with fat and sugar, and our exercise level. Weight is lost only by achieving a calorie deficit, expending more calories than one takes in. In fact, one can lose weight by exercising more and even increasing caloric intake in order to fuel the exercise. The 100 calories burned for every mile run, when totaled over time, is bound to result in significant weight loss, especially if coupled to dietary changes, away from fat and simple sugars and toward lean protein and complex carbs. In short, eat oatmeal and broccoli, not doughnuts and French fries—and work out! It's that simple.

For understandable reasons, nutritionists try to remedy our dietary and lifestyle deficits without addressing the main issues: a fast-food, fatty diet replete with addictive processed foods, and inadequate expenditure of calories at work and play. In our capitalist society, big food joins big automakers, big medicine, and big pharmaceuticals in influencing, even controlling, what we eat, the medicines and supplements we take, and the ways we use and abuse our bodies. Add to that list big diet companies and big fashion, as we discuss in the next chapter.

This is contradictory: we make people sick (or allow them the illusion that they are choosing to be sick) through lifestyles, including diet and leisure, dangerous to them. And then we seek to heal them with supplements, gym memberships, diet pills, and regimes (including 'diet' food delivered to your door), fashion that slims or conceals, and even plastic surgery. The 'commodified' body is harmed and healed by corporate interests who pursue profit above all. **Commodification** involves any good or service being bought and sold in the marketplace. The healing doesn't work because it does not go the heart of the issue: the ensemble of ways we work, play, eat. Although in capitalism the consumer seems to be sovereign, we are provided with spurious choices, and we are influenced to make bad choices through marketing that dominates our **media culture** (Kellner 1995). Pick your poison: Coke, Pepsi, or Red Bull. Raise your hand if you haven't seen an ad for franchised food or diet pills and aids within the last 24 hours?

DISCUSSION QUESTIONS

1. Think back to your last annual physical exam. Did your doctor focus on exercise as a preventive step that you could take to keep yourself healthy? Did he or she discuss your BMI?
2. Do you take supplements to enhance your diet? Do they make you feel better?
3. How many times a day or week do you weigh yourself? How many times a day do you look in the mirror to check your appearance?

IV: Body Industries

Just as we have a number, such as the BMI, for everything, so we try to solve problems by creating markets for cures. Some of these fixes are important; a person with high cholesterol may well need statin drugs that reduce 'bad' cholesterol (LDL). (Vigorous exercise is thought to raise 'good' cholesterol—HDL.) Sometimes cholesterol is impervious to a lean diet, especially where people inherited the cholesterol profile from their parents. But other hokey fixes are simply designed to make someone money. Think of those electronic pulsating belts, advertised in early-morning infomercials, that supposedly firm one's abs and cause one to lose weight! They don't work, but they will make your wallet leaner. And so we need to be skeptical about body industries that purport to solve the human problems of an affluent, high-fructose society.

The Body as Commodity

In our market economy, commodities are any goods or services that are bought and sold; they have a price on them. A new car, a tennis racket, a visit to the physical therapist are all commodities to be transacted. Much has been written about markets, both pro and con. Adam Smith argued that governments should stay out of the interactions of buyers and sellers which would, by themselves, solve all social problems. According to Smith, market exchanges (money for commodities) would benefit all parties, if unequally.

Writing a hundred years after Smith, Karl Marx and Friedrich Engels (2002) agreed with him that markets are vital engines of economic progress. Societies cannot industrialize, and thus satisfy people's basic material needs, without going through a phase of markets, which Marx called capitalism. However, writing with the luxury of hindsight, Marx identified 'contradictions' in the 19th century market economies of European and English capitalism, notably the tendency of the rich to get richer—so rich, in fact, that they would not be able to re-invest their enormous wealth productively, growing the economy and creating jobs. Marx distinguished between wealth (all wealth, including money stuffed into a shoe box for a rainy day) and productive wealth (wealth that breeds more wealth through investment and job creation). He termed this productive wealth capital.

Marx's time was also the time of Charles Dickens, who wrote *A Christmas Carol* in the same year, 1843, that Marx was writing his first book on social philosophy and economics. We all remember the disabled Tiny Tim, whose father, Bob Cratchett, earned a meager wage from his miserly employer Scrooge. Eventually, Scrooge had bad dreams, including visitations from Christmas past, present, and future, that persuaded him to open up his coffers and raise Cratchett's salary, which was being stretched thin to support his large family and pay for Tiny Tim's medical care.

Tiny Tim had body problems, for which he needed treatment. He eventually received proper care because Scrooge saw the light and acted humanely in raising the wage of Tim's father, Bob. Neither Marx nor Dickens systematically considered people's bodies because it was obvious to them that bodies in mid-19th century England and Europe were merely extensions of machines and did not have elaborate needs, beyond food, clothing, and shelter.

Marx never considered that working people would develop what later thinkers (e.g., Marcuse 1964) considered **false needs** for commodities that would not serve their best interests. Marx could not have imagined our media culture, based on advertising and entertainment, any more than he would have foreseen people shopping, using credit cards, beyond their basic needs. Tiny Tim needed clothing and food, while kids today 'need' video games.

Thus, Marx did not foresee body problems based on the body's immersion in the various markets for food, clothing, diets, gym memberships, workout gear, medicine, therapy, massages. The Nike company that Bowerman helped start would have surprised Marx, and probably Adam Smith, too! The impoverished workers in their time would not have understood the need to 'just do it.' They were already 'doing it'— going to work and struggling to survive. They had little leisure time in which to cycle or run. They did not even have Saturdays off. Many of Nikes' shoes and clothing are made off-shore by workers in Third-World countries willing to work far below the American minimum wage. These workers are not worrying about their marathon personal best times.

The bottom line is that there is much money, billions of dollars and Euros, to be made from bodies and the body problems created by these industries. Provoked by advertising, we amuse, abuse, and impoverish ourselves and then we seek to heal ourselves, spending more money. In my own town, a person can spend $60 or more per month on gym memberships (although one can also spend as little as $10 a month at the parks and recreation gyms). And, with our hospitable climate in north Texas, do you even have to belong to a gym in order to work out?!

The body doesn't care where or how it expends calories and raises the heart rate. While, as noted above, the specialized notion of 'exercise' did not exist until late in the 20th century, a few before that, amateur athletes mainly, pursued excellence in sport, often in the form of competitive games such as the Olympics. They often exercised compulsively, or so it seems; I prefer to think of them as finding their muse.

The pedestrian movement in the late 19th and early 20th centuries is an example of this. Here were single-minded calorie burners such as Arthur Newton who walked and ran huge distances, sometimes even the length of continents. In the 1920s and 1930s, races of pedestrians crossed the American continent, and money prizes were awarded.

The cross-country **transcon** races in early 20th century America saw barnstormers running from town to town. There was tremendous civic excitement as people lined the streets to watch these ultramarathon men. This represents the beginning of a shift from amateur involvement in sports and games to their professionalization, which gathered rapid momentum with the spread of network television after World War II. As millions of Americans became 'fans,' they risked a calorie surplus as they sat on their couch viewing and eating but not exercising. As well, professional sports became another huge body industry.

Gyms

I have referred to the first running revolution of the 1970s and early 1980s beginning with Cooper and Bowerman in the 1960s. We are now amid a **second running revolution**, which also includes **crosstraining** and triathlons. Sometimes people cross-train by rotating their exercise pursuits, both preventing injury and staying motivated through diversity. But many do not run at all, preferring 'the gym.' This is new, just as are the terms 'working out' and 'workout,' which mainly refer to gym-based work.

By and large, gyms are compartmentalized by gender. Women use cardio machines, such as ellipticals, while men do resistance training, deploying both free weights and weight machines. To be sure, there is crossover; some women lift and some men do cardio, using ellipticals, treadmills, and stair-steppers. Indeed, both genders use treadmills, just as they use the pavement outside and the floors of shopping malls to walk, a new (but old) form of exercise designed for aging **baby boomers** with creaky knees. And many women who use gyms attend workout classes in which women spin (on stationary bikes), step, or do an all-round 'boot camp' in what amount to support groups with rockin' background music.

The exercise industry pushes gyms over running and walking because there is money to be made in gym memberships. Gyms are often understaffed in order to reduce their overheads; they hope that people will sign up for monthly contracts but not use the gym (hence not depreciating it). However, the sports-clothing industry pushes running and walking where it can profit from selling expensive running shoes and clothing—now called 'technical' clothing to distinguish it from mere cotton or cotton-blend clothing. Nike, Adidas, and Reebok compete for market share among people who run and walk and also among gym users, who can be outfitted in expensive attire.

Some people who sign up for gym memberships do not use them daily or even regularly. But regulars find that driving to the facility and setting aside time to be spent on exercise make the daily workout special. This is inviolable personal time, away from family and work, that has the additional benefit of enhancing fitness and promoting weight loss.

I belong to a gym primarily to use the weight machines. Sometimes I'll crosstrain on the ellipticals or use them to recover from a running injury. Most people sport iPods, which become another expensive exercise accoutrement. The rows of cardio machines and weights make gyms seem like factories, and better bodies are the output.

Weight Loss

Gym memberships peak when people make New Year's resolutions to lose weight and just before swimsuit and wedding season. People join gyms to achieve svelte bodies, although they may also join for cardiac-related reasons. Often, motives are mixed; people want to lose weight but they come to realize that they may actually get bigger as they become more toned, especially if lifting weights. Their body fat may decline and waistline shrink while they stay the same weight or lose or gain a few pounds. By and large, Americans link exercising and body improvement, especially weight loss.

The average American woman believes that she should lose about 16 pounds. This is the sort of woman, not yet morbidly obese, who joins gyms. Such weight loss is manageable with a thrice-weekly workout session, which may also include walking, running, or cycling outdoors. I suspect that most people who visit gyms regularly do not also exercise outside; working out at the gym is their dose of exercise.

Instead of using rapid weight-loss diets and diet pills that merely quicken the metabolism without aerobic benefits, that woman (or man) can lose the 16 pounds simply by building in exercise to her (or his) daily routine. A pound is roughly equivalent to 3,500 calories of stored energy. A mile run equals about 100 calories (depending on weight and speed). If a person runs for 30 minutes (about three miles for many long-slow-distance runners) four times a week, he or she expends an extra 1,200 calories. This assumes no change in one's diet and the number of calories consumed. Typically, an exercise routine will lead people to substitute healthy food for calorie-dense 'junk' food. This new exercise routine (and it could be the elliptical, vigorous walking, cycling, swimming, as well as running) will result in a pound lost every three weeks, simply as a result of extra calories expended. By 48 weeks, one will have lost all of the 16 pounds without embarking on a crash diet that usually fails because it is too depriving. And if one increases the exercise load, the weight will come off even more quickly. Into the bargain, one will have also changed one's lifestyle and one's concept of the 'self.' Looking in the mirror, you will see an athlete, and a healthier, more toned body.

Gyms are only a small slice of the body industry devoted to weight loss. Anyone who watches TV has heard, repeatedly, about Weight Watchers, Nutrisystem, Slim

Fast, Jenny Craig, and the host of other weight-loss programs. These programs combine advice, monitoring, support, and even prepared foods, delivered directly to the home. Celebrities tug at their loose belts and crow about how their waistlines have diminished because of a commercial weight-loss program. Increasingly, male celebrities tout these diets, penetrating a whole new market for diet aids among men who imitate their dieting sports heroes. Many women have always been on board with the equation of slimness and self-worth.

It is not surprising that a society focused on appearance, a certain conception of **masculinity** and **femininity** (as reflected in body shape), and a single-number (positivist) approach to solving problems would spawn the multi-billion dollar weight-loss industry. Weight loss is primarily about the outer shell and not about fitness. To be fair, most contemporary weight-loss programs advise their clients to get regular exercise, recognizing that calorie expenditure is a crucial part of successful weight loss.

Most people who embark on weight-loss diets, especially crash diets, fail. That is, they return to their earlier weights. It is estimated that 95 percent of dieters do not succeed. The 5 percent who manage to keep the pounds off have two common characteristics: they eat breakfast, thus staving off blood-sugar decline later in the day, and they exercise regularly. The exercise might be strenuous and frequent enough that they raise their **metabolic set points**—the rate at which they burn food as fuel. Aerobic exercise, performed conversationally at or above 60/70 percent of maximum heart rate, and weight-lifting have both been found to quicken the metabolism and burn calories after the exercise has ended.

The testimonials in *People* magazine about women who lost 100 pounds or more make for interesting body sociology. Most of the women possess strong will and a goal. Most lost a considerable amount of weight before plateauing, reaching a level of weight lost, say 75 pounds, that they could not exceed. To lose the 75 pounds they combined diet and exercise. The diets did not involve starvation, for that wouldn't give them enough calories to exercise; rather, the diets stressed lean protein, bulky complex carbohydrates, and fat with healthy Omega-3 (as from cold-water fish such as salmon). They ate right, not necessarily less. And they began to work out, often beginning with humble walking routines.

They pushed through their weight-lost plateaus in order to lose a full 100 pounds by increasing the duration and intensity of their exercise. They went from walking a 5K race to running a marathon. They increased their weekly running mileage or aerobic exercise duration using ellipticals and bicycles. It becomes clear in reading these women's narratives that they changed their whole lives, exercised more, ate better, removed sources of stress, and, perhaps most important, began to like themselves more.

Self-esteem is clearly an issue for many women and some men. Sociologically, self-esteem is a product of one's upbringing and also how one measures up to socially acceptable norms (or whether one just ignores those norms). If women measure themselves against nearly anorexic-looking, runway models, they inevitably find themselves wanting. By contrast, men are supposed to be 'big,' even bulky, albeit with firm abs. A study of college women and men's body images (Hesse-Biber 1996), *Am I Thin Enough Yet?*, reveals that most of the college women view themselves as flawed, and overweight, while some college guys want to be bigger. Predictably, eating disorders among the women were rampant, as was compulsive exercising. Presumably, many of the college men got their calories from beer.

This is not to deny that men have their share of body problems, especially where masculinity is tied to being 'big' and muscled. The 2008 movie *Bigger, Faster, Stronger* documents the use of steroids by young men who re-sculpt themselves.

Surgery, Salons, and Fashion

If one watches infomercials at an early hour, as I sometimes do before I go running, one will view a combination of advertisements for diet aids and programs and now, a step beyond, **bariatric surgery**. They will also see ads for medications that address erectile dysfunction (ED), a male body problem possibly related to blood pressure and weight. Bariatric surgery solves body problems for people who are so obese that they cannot lose weight through conventional means, diet and exercise, or, even if they aren't obese, cannot lose the weight and keep it off. And so we address the body problem of obesity surgically.

As well, women and a few men resort to **cosmetic surgery**, nipping and tucking their ways to a perfect body. Everyone has seen examples of cosmetic surgeries that did not work, making the person look like a veteran of military combat. In a society that prizes girl-like female beauty, it is no wonder that aging women want to turn back the clock, much as Hollywood stars have done. Whether these celebrities have achieved rock-hard and slender bodies through exercise and diet or also some cosmetic surgery is an open question to be answered in the tabloids. But our society treats aging women as has-beens, while men who age become 'distinguished' and authoritative. To be sure, there are pressures on men, as well, as we can judge by hair-restoration products and wash-away-the-gray solutions. There is not total gender differentiation here.

Cosmetic surgery also includes breast augmentation, with nipping and tucking now joined by implanting. Why would a woman want bigger boobs?! Because she measures herself against actresses such as Pamela Anderson and feels less-than-fully-feminine with smaller breasts. And femininity and masculinity are socially constructed; there are no inherent and timeless categories of gender identity. A male-dominated culture centers on breasts, and men's penchant for big ones. This has as much to do with the way men construct their gender, acquiring social status from a girlfriend with large breasts, as women construct theirs. Without thinking about breasts as body problems for both women and men, it is otherwise difficult to explain the strange phenomenon of a themed restaurant with the coy name of Hooters.

Women address their body problems through a host of measures such as diet, exercise, cosmetic and/or bariatric surgery. They also use traditional means such as regular visits to salons and hairdressers and attention to trends in fashion (especially now that we have the phenomenon of **vanity sizing**, discussed below).

To be feminine, many women have their hair done properly and regularly coiffed. For many women, this also involves dying, streaking, and tinting. A local hairdresser in urban Dallas estimated to me that no local woman over the age of 40 fails to 'restore' her hair! This is Texas, the land of big hair and traditional femininity. I would add that many women under 40 have their hair colored, just as they acquire tattoos and piercings—body alterations that fall under the rubric of cosmetic surgery (or that, in the case of tattoos, bridge surgery and tinting). These piercings and tattoos contribute to the impression that the person is youthful and perhaps sexually available.

At salons women have their hair and nails done. Hair work often includes dying and may include perming, depending on the style of the moment. Manicuring and pedicuring may be purchased at a specialty store or at a full-service salon. Millions are spent by women on nail care; and, like hair, this is a self-reproducing industry. Nice-looking nails fade and chip and must be restored. Just how we have included painted nails in our repertoire of 'femininity' is a curious historical question. For those of us who came of age during the hippie sixties, or even those today who live in hip bastions such as Eugene, Oregon, and Santa Fe, New Mexico, all of this cosmetic body altering is so mainstream and fifties-ish! In these still-countercultural sites, women are proud to have long gray hair and unadorned nails. Just driving the few hours from Santa Fe to Texas sends one backward (or forward?) in time, from hippieville to big hair, red nails, and boob jobs. Variation in patterns and practices of femininity along Interstate 40 suggests the inherently flexible, even arbitrary standards of femininity and masculinity. (In Santa Fe and Eugene, it is common to see men with pony tails, whereas in Texas men often resemble Marines.)

Hair and nails are, in effect, elements of fashion; they adorn the clothed female body. One moves from being female to being feminine by attending to these 'extras.' The line between **body work** (dieting, hair, nails, cosmetic surgery) and fashion is blurry. Hair and nails are fashion statements in their own right. However, clothing is a peculiar type of body work that conceals parts of the body, either cloaking what must not be seen or drawing attention away from body parts viewed as flawed.

Most people find flaws in their body. My feet are too flat. Clothing conceals body work, such as gym work and surgery, where it has failed to achieve its purpose. Or, if a woman has lost weight and gotten toned, she may choose fashions which highlight these new aspects. Fashion is a way of resolving body problems, either by concealing, distracting, or emphasizing. So-called vanity sizing responds to the growing American body shape. Stores vanity size where they portray what used to be a size 8 as a size 6, flattering its wearer and suggesting that she is 'smaller' than she is.

The fashion industry, immensely profitable and influential, is quite postmodern; it lacks firm coordinates of style but changes with the season. The word 'fashion' suggests ever-changing standards. One year the flip (hair) is in vogue, where next year women sport long, curled hair. Last year, flip flops, this year Roman sandals. There is no logic to this and designers risk running out of trends. **Postmodernism** (Harvey 1989; Agger 2002) is an artistic and architectural movement that blends old and new, for example embellishing modernist, rectangular skyscrapers with architectural signatures from the medieval or early-modern period.

Postmodernism (Lyotard 1984) is also a philosophy of history that questions whether we are moving forward progressively in a straight line toward a perfect world. The fashion industry can scarcely be called philosophical, but it is eclectic, borrowing from here and there in order to convince women buyers to re-clothe themselves every season. Even the most skeptical of women, to fit in and get ahead, gesture toward these fashion trends, whether they have public jobs or work at home. The **fashionista** takes fashion trends seriously, much like the **foodie** takes foods and restaurants seriously (see Johnston and Baumann 2009). But these trends are essentially arbitrary.

And in the case of fashion they are established mainly by men, who rule the fashion industry. Fashion is not about art, except, perhaps, for **haute couture**—the expensive one-of-a-kind frocks purchased by the rich. **Prêt-à-porter** (off-the-rack, ready-to-wear) for the mass millions is simply another assembly line, making high fashion accessible to the middle class but risking duplication, even a risk in haute couture where we see actresses pictured in popular magazines wearing the same outfit. We then 'vote' to decide which actress or model we prefer in a certain Dior.

Not only are fashions arbitrary, with short skirts one season and flowing ones the next; the very notion of seasonality is arbitrary. Why not five-year cycles, within which there would be a degree of consensus about what's 'in' and 'out'? The answer is economic; the more rapidly in/out changes, the more purchasing will take place. Corporate fashion might respond that fickle women are stimulated by novelty. But that is surely an outcome and not a cause; they are led to expect fashion trends and assume that they will have to shop every season, year-in and year-out.

What body problem does fashion solve? Feminists would answer 'self-esteem.' That is, most women are taught to measure themselves in the mirror against the images of Demi Moore and Gisele Bundchen. Even body stars are flawed in conventional terms. We know and see them only through the idealizing lens of the camera. They use makeup, hair, nails, gym work, personal training, and maybe even surgical makeovers to produce the image of their own perfection. The average woman cannot or will not go this far, but nevertheless she feels that she does not measure up. For most working women and men, who labor for the average 40 hours a week and have families and commute to work, there is precious little time left over for self-care, let alone money for makeovers.

Even watching the news can be disheartening, as attractive anchor people chat merrily about their own family and work obligations, with perfect makeup and thoughtful attire. Fashion is merely one vehicle among many of the idealization of feminine beauty; it raises the bar on the feminine ideal, but the bar is so high as to be unattainable. Again, there is a gap between what we see on the screen or on the fashion runway and what we would see if we really rubbed shoulders with celebrities living their own everyday lives on Rodeo Drive in Los Angeles. They would appear frumpy by comparison to their glossy images on Oscar night. They would be us!

And so body industries designed to resolve body problems caused by a fast-food society may actually cause problems, especially psychic ones, as most people fall short. Weight-loss diets frequently fail; work-like gym work and personal training are time-consuming and can be expensive; fashion fails to raise self-esteem because 'we' don't look like 'them,' our cultural role models.

DISCUSSION QUESTIONS

1. Do you work out? How many times a week, and what are your exercises? Do you belong to a gym? Does this make you feel better?
2. How many times have you tried to lose weight? List the diets you have tried, and discuss whether they worked to get and keep the weight off.
3. At gyms and road races today, women equal or outnumber men. Why did women join the exercise revolution? Do we have to change our definition of femininity now that many women are athletes?

V: Beyond Body Work

T he American debate over health care rages on. President Obama is trying to reform a cumbersome and expensive health care system that leaves some people out. But his critics argue that he is trying to legislate 'socialized medicine,' which, for many Americans, has a scary sound to it. Few believe that government inside the Washington, D.C. beltway can efficiently solve the local problems of Americans.

Those of us who support universal health care as a basic human right, enjoyed by most Europeans, must respond to the idea that there are lots of obese, unhealthy people whose inactive and high-calorie lifestyles make them sick. Should 'healthy' people support people who make poor consumer and health choices? Shouldn't people bear some responsibility for their wellness? A sociologist might respond that advertising is so powerful, especially when it targets youngsters, that people cannot easily make autonomous rational choices. Scholars attempt to explain the anomaly that poor people waste their money on fast food, which makes them fat and drains their resources. They point to advertising and to the absence, in low-income urban areas, of affordable and healthy food.

And so we conclude this book with considerations of what society might do for people with body problems, and what people might do for themselves. I take issue with the medical model of body problems, even as we can learn from it. And I raise questions about whether even 'exercise' conceived as body work and not as self-creative play is a solution.

I return to my earlier discussion of the medical model of body problems as we attempt to surpass it (without relinquishing all of its benefits). **De-medicalizing the body** will not put physicians and physical therapists out of business. Even an experienced runner cannot diagnose a stress fracture in the hip or foot; one must consult the x-ray or bone scan. But the diagnosis of a stress fracture need not lead to lengthy and expensive dependence on a physical therapist; the injured athlete can learn his or her own rehab, either from a brief visit to a physical therapist or by doing one's own research. I once went to a chiropractor who insisted that I sign up for 20 visits before even knowing whether his therapy would work. Suspicious of the medical model and not wanting to waste the limited number of visits allowed by my insurance, I healed myself by doing Internet research on how to rehab my sports injury of the moment. What really helped—and this cost nothing—was rest!

Exercise or Play?

With what do we replace, or augment, the medical model in dealing with body problems? The answer is multi-part:

- Overthrow Cartesian dualism and stress mind–body unity.
- View the person as an agent and not simply a patient or a consumer.
- Stress the health benefits of physical activity viewed as play and not work.
- Focus on children and build an hour a day of strenuous movement into the curriculum.
- De-emphasize athletic competition viewed as a zero-sum or winner/loser contest; everyone wins.
- Move toward a society in which people 'play' not only with their bodies but also their minds, dis-alienating work now viewed as a calling and not simply a means to an economic end.

The body cannot be isolated from the surrounding society and from nature. We are sentient people; that is, we are connected to the world through our bodies and our senses. Descartes and other philosophical dualists erred by disembodying human consciousness, thus allowing later utopians (theorists of the good society) to portray modernity in ways that sacrifice the working/exercising body in return for economic gains. A stark image is of the stressed-out business person who works long hours, eats on the run (and drive), and enjoys little leisure time. He or she amasses a fortune but dies young from cardiac problems such as strokes and heart attacks. A deep question is whether it is worth the sacrifice.

My personal perspective is that there needs to be time to smell (and plant) the roses. No work is worth doing unless it expresses oneself. Work must answer to a calling, whether painting, poetry, or auto mechanics. We must blur the sharp boundary drawn by philosophers such as Immanuel Kant between the spheres of work and leisure or freedom. We must conceive of work as free and we must make it free, just as we need to create leisure opportunities that do not emphasize indolence, inactivity, simply recovery from back-breaking and boring labor.

The problem with exercise as a panacea for everything, all the way from high blood pressure to depression, is that exercise typically occupies a small compartment in people's busy lives. And it can become a job whose output is gauged by various metrics such as elapsed time, weight pumped, calories expended, number of repetitions and sets. Many body workers are advised by their personal trainers to keep a journal or log. Exercise is more than the expenditure of energy. It is a communion with the body, a seeking of unity between mind and body, **flow**, life lived in the **zone**.

As compulsive and work-oriented people, runners too often view their own activity as body work, with miles counted, intervals timed, running logs filled, races run, and medals won. I'm no stranger to this compulsion, as my occasional flirtation with **overtraining** reveals. I am not suggesting that one's communion with the body must involve running; any activity that raises the heart rate and consumes large amounts of oxygen is worth doing. It could be walking, cycling, rowing, or dancing.

Running is hard, even when done gently. When one races, it can really hurt. But, drawing on the work of Johan Huizinga (1950), *Homo Ludens*, I view these activities as play—they are chosen freely and they express the self. Huizinga suggests that we are by nature playful; we express ourselves through our games and physical pursuits. This play pushes the limits; it is not always comfortable. Racing involves effort and suffering, especially after the first mile. At the end, one is spent, doubled over, and panting for oxygen. Why would rational people do this to themselves? For many of us, we cannot stay away. I've been racing for 30 years and I periodically take time off and just do my daily running. But something calls me back to the starting line, surrounded by other playful ascetics who express themselves through their hard running. I suppose I love the running that prepares me for race day, even as I get injured running intervals and then need to back off. Racing is a test. Yet so is hard training that prepares one to race. The cliché is true; everyone who lines up at the start is a winner. And yet many are there just to complete the race, while a few hard-bitten runners are racing themselves, pursuing **PRs (personal records)** but perhaps really pursuing themselves. Hard effort may be a window on the soul or at least on the self. Perhaps effort opens the window.

Call this addiction, whether or not it involves racing. I'm addicted to movement, seeking the flow I have talked about. I know that drugs are involved—endorphins, serotonin, and other neurotransmitters. I might be lethargic, and not my own best friend, were it not for this daily habit which leaves me feeling better not only about my body but about everything. Athlete is the name we give to anyone who stimulates his or her heart and gulps oxygen. But I am not a body worker. This is pure recreation, and more important than any job.

Is Walking Exercise?

A key part of the second running revolution is the participation of baby boomers (born between about 1947 and 1960), who were in their twenties during the first revolution. A graying population dominates road races, producing the effect that marathon times for the average (but older) runner have slowed considerably. In addition, the standard road-running distance of the 1970s, the 10K, has given way to the 5K, a more manageable distance for new runners, fitness runners, and walkers. And the full marathon (26.2 miles) has been matched or even exceeded in popularity by 'the half' (13.1 miles).

A second major change between the first and second revolutions is the massive involvement of women in exercise and fitness. Just as races are now dominated by we elders, so women often outnumber men at every running distance from the 5K to the half. And at road races we now find many walkers, predominantly women. And they hit the roads and neighborhoods after men head off to work and kids have been taken to school.

Is walking exercise? In an obvious sense, it is. Bodies are in motion. And calories are being burned. But burning calories does not necessarily stress the heart sufficiently to produce the training effect, which is usually achieved at between 60 and 100 percent of one's maximum heart rate. This training effect stresses and strengthens the heart and vascular system, producing the diminishing resting heart rate I discussed earlier (see Noakes 2003).

For those who need numbers against which to measure the efficacy of their exercise, here is a trusty formula for determining whether they are getting the 'training effect'—strengthening the cardio-vascular system. Subtract your age from the number 220. Then subtract your resting heart rate. Multiply that number by a number in the range between 0.6 and 1.0. Add back in your age, and you have your target heart-rate range during exertion at which you get the training effect—60 percent to nearly 100 percent of your maximum capacity. **Long slow distance (LSD)** is running between about 60 and 75 percent. So-called **tempo running** (anaerobic-threshold running) is done between about 75 and 85 percent, and anaerobic running (intervals) is running above about 85 percent. Most of one's miles should be in the long-slow-distance range, providing plenty of recovery while enhancing endurance, with, at most, a session or two per week of the quicker stuff. Resting heart rate is best measured upon waking or at rest during the day, and exertional heart rate can be easily measured using an inexpensive Polar heart-rate monitor consisting of a chest strap and a watch-like monitor. Now the fancier GPS watches (e.g., Garmin Forerunner) not only monitor heart rate but also distance covered!

There is no free lunch: the most-often injured runners are rookies (who overdo it) and high-mileage veterans (who also overdo it), especially those who add speed work. Time off, including 'easy' days on which people run but get **relative rest**, is the solution. I'm as guilty as the next injured runner when it comes to inhabiting that razor's edge between fitness and getting hurt. My best performances are often preceded by rest, but followed by injury and burnout. Roger Bannister, the first human to break the four-minute mile barrier, in 1954, did not run a step for five days before his record-setting run. Bannister was a medical student interested in the exercise–physiological issue of how to balance stress and rest. This approach focuses on heart rate as a measure of both exertion and fitness.

This razor's edge is where fast people dwell. It is, as Colorado distance coach Mark Wetmore called it, paraphrasing Tom Wolfe, an Edge City where the hardy go to train. They push the envelope, trying to see how much they can take. A season in the life of the University of Colorado cross-country team, coached by Wetmore, reveals his Lydiard-like approach to high mileage and the 'density' of training; his guys have easy days, but even they are hard. They are always pushing to break through to the other side, where excellence and maximum potential are found. But Chris Lear (2003) also chronicles the broken bodies on the side of the road, felled by overuse and stress fractures.

And so whether walking is exercise really depends on whether one's pace and fitness combine to produce the training effect. People walking fast uphill are probably raising the heart rate into the 70 percent or higher range. I raced an eight-miler recently and was struck by how many walkers, mainly women, were motoring quickly and even challenging slower runners late in the race. And now many people, and not only gray-ing ones, combine running and walking, enabling themselves to achieve goals important to them such as completing a marathon. The former elite marathoner and now marathon coach Jeff Galloway argues that one should break up long runs with regular stints of walking, thus resting and rejuvenating the legs. And people who run **ultra-marathons** (more than 26.2 miles, even as far as 50 or 100 miles) have long known that ultra runners must take periodic walking breaks, especially late in the race. Tom Osler (1980), an ultramarathoner, was one of the first to recommend this. The early pedestrians such as Newton combined walking and running as do most contemporary 'transcon' runners.

The beauty of vigorous walking is that its footstrike is much less stressful than the running footstrike because the runner is defying gravity by lifting the body off the ground. This is basic physics: runners' bodies must absorb more shock, returned to them after crashing to earth, than walkers, cyclists, and swimmers who don't defy gravity in the way runners do.

Running and Being

During the first running revolution, a poet emerged. His name was Dr. George Shee-han, a cardiologist who had become a smoker and strayed from his collegiate run-ning days. In order to address both his smoking and drinking, Sheehan in his forties returned to running, this time mainly on the roads and not the track. He trained prodigiously and raced often. He began to write a column for a small New Jersey paper, an essay really, on how running was affecting his life positively. Sheehan was a wordsmith capable of crafting an elegant phrase. He was also widely read and larded his essays with evocative phrases from great thinkers such as Ralph Waldo Emerson.

Sheehan leaned heavily on Emerson, who said that people should be "good animals" and get in touch with their bodies through hard effort. Above all, Sheehan was anti-Cartesian; he ran, therefore he was. Running became a metaphor of life for Sheehan.

Sheehan's most popular book was (1978) *Running and Being*, a purposely pomp-ous title denoting the esteem in which Sheehan held running. An Irishman, Sheehan viewed life as both joyful and tragic, a combination mimicked in the road race, where each succeeding mile brings one closer to death but also to the release of finishing.

Reaching the finish line was to be followed by drinking something cold and by good fellowship, re-connecting the lonely long-distance runner with his fellow man and woman.

Sheehan lived a vigorous life, doctoring, running, writing, and loving. Although a physician, he did not favor the medical model and preferred to listen to his body. Sometimes, the body cannot be heard and the standard quantitative measures of health need to be heeded. Ironically, when visiting Dr. Kenneth Cooper at his aerobics institute in Dallas, Sheehan learned, too late, that he had cancer and eventually he died from it, but he kept running nearly until the end. Characteristically, Sheehan wrote honestly about dying, a powerful book (1996) entitled *Going the Distance*. It was a book about running, but also about his life and family, which Sheehan sometimes ignored in his lonely pursuit of miles spent on the road. The book revealed that Sheehan had been humbled by his own mortality.

Given his demons, which led to smoking, drinking, and infidelity, and certainly because of his Irish sense of tragedy, I read Sheehan as running-away and not running-toward. Many use running and other forms of exercise to escape a hum-drum everyday life. Running can be that, certainly. But one can also run toward a destination that is the self, one's self. Sheehan learned hard lessons about himself through his miles, as many of us have. We learn about our compulsions, resilience, and desire. You don't need to run to know these things. You can learn them at the gym, on the bike path, practicing the violin—any difficult activity that requires one's undivided and regular attention.

Sheehan speculates that runners are loners; running calls them, us really, as an escape from the madding crowd. But he learns as he dies that even runners need community; they need love. In this sense, running is running-toward those who await us at the finish line and who run next to us. We are always alone, and yet we never are. This is one of the deepest mysteries of the human condition.

By the second running revolution, younger runners do not have much time for Sheehan's musings. To them, running is about fitness, performance, and buff bodies. Perhaps this is a generational shift. The Japanese novelist, Haruki Murakami (2008), wrote a memoir that doubles as a running journal. *What I Talk About When I Talk About Running* was written by a person from my generation, a running-rev **Gen One** person, who links the discipline necessary to run and to write. At the risk of sounding like my father, I wonder if younger runners have the same orientation to hard work and hard racing!

One of the differences between running-rev Gen One and **Gen Two** people is that the former were Lydiard-like high milers, while the latter tend to be low mileage people. Many from Gen One are also participants in Gen Two; we are simply older and cannot handle 70 miles a week and long runs of 20 or more. And, today, there are many neophyte runners who simply want to finish a marathon, and do weeks of 40 with long runs of 16, hoping to run/walk the marathon in six hours. We hard-corers from Gen One did not want only to finish; we raced the distance, hoping to break three hours. I forever regret, although I accept, that I was seven minutes shy of that! With the wisdom afforded to the aged, with hindsight in a word, I might have done a few things differently, even though I ran many big weeks with longs between 20 and 24. I always thought that sub-three was a magical barrier, a dream, really. I now know that achieving it wouldn't have changed my life. Or, rather, by trying I was forever changed. After completing my first marathon I remember that I inhabited my body and trod upon the earth differently. My step was lighter.

The Tarahumara

People often yearn for the good ol' days, which were often not that good. Memory distorts and idealizes. And yet yesteryear exists in the present, as a quick look at a global map reveals many cultures that have not entered 'modernity.' Many, both here and abroad, do not live in cities, drive cars, eat fast food, use the Internet, or rely on service providers for help with their problems. Like the Tarahumara, a Mexican Indian tribe, they exist before modern time and its linear narrative of progress. And the Tarahumara run, often very long distances. For generations, they have chased their prey to ground, pursuing them for hundreds of miles until the animals overheat and succumb.

A recent cult classic among runners, *Born to Run* (McDougall 2009), documents the 'ultramarathoning' exploits of these natural high-altitude pedestrians. Avoiding paved roads by sticking to trails, and often running barefoot or in flimsy sandals without high-tech running clothes, these runners spawned legends that the author Christopher McDougall investigated. Leading American ultramarathoners such as Scott Jurek and Jenn Shelton traveled to Mexico to run with and race Tarahumara legends, who had already competed successfully in 50- and 100-milers on American soil.

In a 100-mile race, such as the very challenging Western States race, runners traverse a narrow trail, littered with natural obstacles such as stumps, boulders, and streams, over often-mountainous terrain.

They run through the night with headlamps and may finish in over 24 hours. Although there are aid stations for food and drink, much of the race is done alone. Toward the end of the race some ultra runners use pacers, for companionship and moral support. Walking is interspersed with running. Consider that many marathoners complete their 26.2 mile races, contested over smooth and well-tended pavement, in four hours. If they drop out, they are close to home. And rarely do their courses have huge changes in elevation and climate.

The existence of the Tarahumara and of other aboriginal running cultures suggests that people were indeed 'born to run,' in order to capture their food. Running amid nature, without over-engineered shoes over cement surfaces, came naturally to hunter—gatherer societies. Running answers to our genetic need for self-propelled movement.

Figure 5.1 Jenn Shelton, Scott Jurek, and Ian Torrence running a trail ultra.

And this sort of long-distance running necessarily blurred the boundary between running (slowly) and walking (fast). These natural runners are, in the parlance of earlier cross-continental runners, 'pedestrians.' They go places on their feet.

Why do people engage in these 'ultra' feats, and also triathlons, adventure racing, and other extreme activities? Consider the Badwater ultramarathon. It covers 135 miles and takes runners through Death Valley, with temperatures in the 120s, and then ascends Mount Whitney, with cold and snow. Runners could not survive without 'handlers' who trail them in campers and provide them with water and food. This is time spent in purgatory, again begging the question 'why?' And there is an even sicker race called the Barkley, a 100-miler through extreme terrain in Tennessee on an unmarked trail. Visit http://run100miles.com/race-reports/the-barkley-marathons for a glimpse of that madness.

My answer involves Descartes, he of the split self–mind and body. The standard answer, which also may have validity, is that such extreme running gives their lives meaning, as if they need to run. This is the perspective of George Sheehan, who reclaimed his own life and family through running. But the Tarahumara are not running away from boring lives. They find running to be 'natural,' something people just do. Why wouldn't they be content to run just a few miles? For one, their prey can't be run to ground that quickly. Also, I think we are driven to achieve a certain sensation of mind–body unity, of flow, as exercise theorists call it. This unity or flow derives from the ineffable feeling of movement, of the body taking over and effortlessly moving down the road. A participant in the positive-psychology movement with Seligman, Mihaly Csikszentmihalyi (1990) has addressed flow from a psychological perspective. For him, flow derives from being fully immersed in the task at hand. Richard Davidson (Weil 2006) has examined the MRIs of Tibetan monks after they have meditated in exploring ways of achieving unity or flow. He finds that meditation actually changes brain functioning. Meditation is apparently one way of getting there; mine is running, although the rhythmic breathing involved in running long and clearing one's mind of clutter is, for all practical purposes, a kind of meditation!

Sometimes exercise-physiology experts call this being in the zone. But zone implies that most of the time doing sports is spent outside of it, when the baseball does not look as big as a grapefruit or the miles do not click by effortlessly. Experienced runners are often in this zone, experiencing mind–body unity as soon as they warm up in the first few miles. Some speculate that runners experience a high, but this is not exactly the same thing as flowing. **Runner's high** may simply indicate a one-degree rise in body temperature after one runs a mile or so and breaks a sweat. Others speculate that very long efforts release endorphins and other neurotransmitters that produce an opiate-like effect (see Bergland 2007). This can even occur at short distances.

Being in the zone? Flowing? Floating on a runner's high? These may be different ways of describing a post-Cartesian experience of seamless meshing between the mind and body. The legs feel like they have a mind of their own and the runner need not exert will to produce the effect of motion. Arthur Lydiard, the New Zealand coach of legend, may have the key to all of this: his months-long period of base building (accumulating many miles as the runner approaches his or her aerobic capacity), when followed by the few weeks of sharpening, achieved through speed work, can seem to give the legs and body an independent will. One simply wants to move forward fast, and this fast running is nearly effortless, supported by the months of endurance work.

Is it only motion, though, that produces flow, the unification of mind and body I am talking about? After decades of running, racing, injuries, rethinking, I believe that flow or unity is half the story. The other half involves oxygen, consumed in very large amounts for hours on end. This is the core of the term 'aerobic'—exercising with the aid of sufficient oxygen. Breathing oxygen when we run and live allows the conversion of fuel into energy, which enables our muscles to fire. This is basic exercise science. But these massive amounts of oxygen, ingested regularly, produce a feeling of well-being that partly accounts for the experience of flow. I almost never experience flow in the first mile of a run. It takes longer, sometimes into the second hour. The problem for a runner at my advanced age is that the lure of the second hour is a siren song leading me to my demise—injuries and overtraining! If I discipline myself to run long only once a week or every other week, I preserve my ability to keep doing this. Actually, I find that speed work and racing break me down more than does long slow distance, as Joe Henderson (1969, 1976) called it.

Sheehan approaches this matter mystically. He believed that the truth of life is revealed to trained runners. As we will see when we discuss the transcon runner James Shapiro later, the truth is that there is only process, not a final destination. My own temperament leads me to agree with him. But Lydiard's exercise–physiological framework, with base building followed by sharpening work, may be equally convincing. And then there is another explanation, deriving flow from the enhancement of opiate-like neurotransmitters that trigger a sort of euphoria, or at least lead to addiction.

One question is why Scott Jurek, Jenn Shelton, and the Tarahumara run over mountains through the night, knowing they will never appear on ESPN or make millions. Another might be why runners who run nearly every day do so for years on end, regardless of the weather outside, their injuries, fatigue, or the demands of their busy lives. Is this compulsion or play? Perhaps the motivations are the same. They seek flow as well as euphoria as well as oxygen, the feeling of effortless movement, but this is hard-won. It does not come at first, to beginners or even weekend warriors. And it only comes to people who put 'process' ahead of 'outcome,' that is, who love the feeling of motion, hour upon hour, even though they may also like going fast and racing. I have my reasons for racing, such as placing in my age group! But nothing compares to the 13-milers done in the dark under a harvest moon, when mist rises from the field and stream, the air feels cool on my chest, and the legs just take me.

I return from these long runs refreshed and ready for more. But at my age the risk of overtraining is real. Not just a casual term for overdoing it, overtraining is a set of physical symptoms such as a fall-off in performance, fatigue, a raised pulse, weakened resistance to colds. It took me years to learn that the most important part of running is not the running but the rest, the off-days that should come once a week and, sometimes, need to occupy a whole week so that I can get the soreness out of my legs and fall in love again with the feeling of motion. It is easy for those addicted to flow to get so beaten up that they crawl, not fly!

Running or other aerobic activity is not a panacea for several reasons: bodies break down and these activities must be taken in manageable doses; Lydiard advised runners to return from every run feeling that he or she could have done more. "Train, don't strain," was his motto. As well, the tendency for all human pursuits to be 'commodified' affects running no less than fashion, video games, music. Runners are not outside of the world, immune to the lure of advertising. We easily believe that the newest 100-dollar running shoes will make us faster or that running tights will actually prevent injury. Or that the right physical therapist can keep us going forever. Well, Dr. Griffin probably can, he who purveys **active release therapy** (**ART**), a magic technique.

I'm a low-tech or even no-tech person. I'll run in any old clothing, whether it is officially for runners or not. As for fuel, give me apple or orange juice over Gatorade any day; I'll take a peanut butter and jelly sandwich over a so-called energy bar (candy bar by any other name) or GU (a disgusting gel that one takes, with water, on the run). Gatorade is just water, sugar, and some electrolytes (e.g., potassium) that can be had in regular beverages.

I've drunk my share of Gatorade (the powdered kind is much cheaper than the bottled), and will again, no doubt. It is convenient because it is everywhere. But Gatorade is a good example of corporate interest run amok. They fund studies supposedly proving that dehydration is lurking around every corner, ready to send the runner or athlete into heat distress and possibly death. But we now find that slow runners, taught to drink even when they are not thirsty, are collapsing and even dying because of **hyponatremia**, a word for water intoxication—having drunk too much at every aid station while running and/or walking a slow marathon.

Exercise science (Tucker, Dugas, and Fitzgerald 2009) now holds that people should drink when thirsty, perhaps (Noakes 2003) preceded, just before a stint of hour-or-more exercise in hot weather, by water. In a long trail race I even re-fueled with Coke, getting sugars, water, and carbs!

American doctors, prodded by Gatorade and other corporate hydrators, have backed away from the tough-guy mentality of earlier generations, when drinking water while exercising was a sign of weakness; they have set guidelines suggesting that people should drink whenever possible, even if they aren't thirsty. This is an example of the corporate influence of health standards. Given the newfound risk of water intoxication, we are now moving to a more flexible standard of drinking at will. Another example is the effort, by some physicians, to lower the boundary demarcating high from healthy blood pressure from 140/90 to 120/80, even where the medical research supporting this may be scanty. Such a move is supported by drug companies who sell millions of dollars of anti-hypertension medication and who now want to define more potential customers as having borderline high blood pressure that needs to be medicated.

It is now accepted by many that people, not necessarily athletes, require 64 ounces of water a day for good health. This breaks down into eight bottles of corporate water. But no scientific evidence supports this. Most people are probably adequately hydrated, even if they haven't yet made their philanthropic contributions to Ozarka or Evian. These are examples of how we solve body problems supposedly using the medical model ('sciences' of dehydration and hypertension) but, in fact, we are only lining corporate pockets and, in the case of hydration, risking water intoxication.

I am not saying that Gatorade and Ozarka are bad products, even though Gatorade is probably light on sugar (see Noakes 2003). (Dehydration won't get you—the runner—but low fuel probably will in long efforts unless you eat on the run.) I am suggesting that public-health standards are influenced by the drive for corporate profit. Running shoe and apparel companies are no different. They sell shoes as if shoes alone will prevent running injuries. There is a movement toward **barefoot running** (or running with minimalist footwear, such as Vibram Five Fingers and Nike Frees) which liberates the foot altogether, an approach promoted in McDougall's book on the Tara-humara, who also run in minimal or no footwear.

Meditations from the Breakdown Lane

All is not sweetness and light for the endurance athlete. Consider an ultra of 100 miles, a very long effort compared with a 26.2 marathon. And now multiply this by 30; that is the effort needed to cross the country, about 3,000 miles worth of running. It is estimated that fewer than a 100 people have completed transcons. I discuss three who have attempted them, James Shapiro, Charlie Engle, and Katie Visco, and explore their motivations and experiences on the run.

When I was running marathons, back in the late seventies and early eighties, a young man named James Shapiro, a Harvard grad who was into Zen Buddhism, decided to run from California to his hometown of New York City. It was not a casual decision. Shapiro was an experienced ultra runner, and he could run 40 miles or more at a stretch. He had completed 100-milers and he had a good idea that a transcon was a serious effort, not to be trifled with. He charted a course carefully, because much of his run would be 'solo' and he needed to know where he could find shelter in towns along the way. And he reckoned with the prospect of running about 40 miles a day for 80 days, with only the occasional day off.

We who run seriously recognize the problem: recovery. In my prime, I could run 26 miles, but only after 80-mile weeks and weekly runs in the 20s. After the marathon itself, especially if I raced it, I would need to recuperate, even walking down stairs backwards! Here Shapiro was planning to go the distance, and more, each and every day for months on end.

He wrote a book about his effort, *Meditations from the Breakdown Lane* (1983). Although out of print, the book is available in the used-book market and in libraries. I have read my copy many times for 30 years, dipping into it periodically for inspiration. I am inspired by Shapiro's gumption and his tolerance of suffering. I am drawn to his introspection about his own motives. He comes to realize, perhaps with the help of his Zen framework, that the transcon is not about getting from there to here, from California to his home base in NYC. Shapiro learns that he is always 'home,' held up by the world and even helped by random people on his route. He is never alone, nor lonely, even as the run wears on and he craves company, comfort, an end to it all.

His book, and his experience, are all about process, not outcomes. As he begins his effort, he is overwhelmed by the fact that he has a very long way to go. Each day is so strenuous that to envisage 70 more of them would be too depressing. He forces himself to stay 'in the moment.' Plodding along from town to town, he marks his passage by half-inches covered on his well-creased maps. Even to leave the state of California, which takes several days, is an arrival of sorts, just as he takes note of the fact that eventually he must leave the West for the relatively dense civilization of the Midwest, especially if you count the cows and other livestock!

By Ohio and then Pennsylvania, he is just tuckered out. He ups his daily mileage in order to get home, even as he is mildly depressed that the effort has to end. This is the biggest adventure of his life, as it would be for anyone. Even as he writes a book about his adventure, he cannot quite believe that he did the run. It was like a dream.

What did Shapiro learn? He learned that everywhere there is ground and sky anchoring him in the present. He gives up the concept of 'destination' in favor of process—just awakening to the sun and birdsong and hitting the road. After a few weeks of life on the road, spent as "road hog" or "road fox," he reports that he has learned not to worry about where he will stay that night. Things always work out, even though he sometimes resents having to cover big chunks of territory simply to find a motel. He says he enjoys the wide open spaces and even desolation of the West, but he relaxes when he hits the Midwest and realizes that towns are close together and the next meal and bed are always just around the corner.

Compare Shapiro's experience to that of Katie Visco (2010. http://www.paveyour-lane.com), a 24-year-old woman who recently graduated from Carleton College. On December 29, 2009, she set foot in the Pacific Ocean at San Diego, having run all the way from Boston. It took her exactly nine months to make her way west. At the time she finished in San Diego, she became the second youngest woman ever to complete a transcon. Although she didn't do daily 40s, she put in a good 18 on average, split up into three segments each day, followed by some walking in order to cool down and avoid sore muscles. Just before the end of her trek, Katie was struck by knee pain and had to walk most of the last 300 miles, which was the hardest part of her journey. After her transcon, she began traveling the country talking to kids about her amazing feat, and empowering others, especially young people, to dream big and follow their passions.

And then there is Charlie Engle who, with Ray Zahab and Kevin Lin, ran over 4,000 miles across the Sahara Desert! Their 100-plus day journey was captured on film in a stirring movie, *Running the Sahara*, the best running/anthropology movie I've ever seen. (See http://www.runningthesahara.com.) Recently, Engle attempted his own transcon, with Marshall Ulrich, which was also captured on film (http://www.runningamerica08.com).

How many people would have the audacity to explore life in the breakdown lane? Try running a couple of hours, across town, to the city limits. Find a motel and in the morning set out for the next county. Then multiply that by many hundreds, up and down hills and mountains, through desert, in rain and snow. The isolation would be intimidating, even with a handler driving alongside. I would be overawed by the sheer snail-like pace of the project; Shapiro recalls taking forever to get through Nebraska, one of our widest states. And, as the three runners learned, injury lurks at every turn, jumping out of a bush unbidden to halt the run. Just as Visco limped home, Shapiro

Figure 5.2 Katie Visco runs across Arizona.
Source: Used with permission of Jenny Sadler.

broke down in Iowa, where an emergency-room doctor declared that he must wait a week with his foot elevated in order to beat a devilish infection probably picked up by a combination of dirty, sweaty socks and a tiny burr that pierced the skin around the ankle. And Engle hobbled the last miles from Cairo to the Red Sea, grimacing as his giant blister made locomotion an agonizing act.

The burr almost halted Shapiro, nearly defeating him in the way vast distance could not. He had to dodge traffic on narrow bridges and fight dehydration in the arid western desert. And he had to log huge daily distance in order to get home before winter. I've never read anything written by him since, but one can imagine that he would have been changed by this venture, as Visco and Engle have been, too. As a runner, but not of the ultra kind, it is hard to imagine coming out the other end; I think daily running changes you, hardening, wearing down, giving perspective, if you're lucky affording the unity of flow.

Flow might be another term for freedom; other philosophers call it authenticity or perhaps the absence of alienation. A great many people are alienated, from their jobs, the natural world, their fellows, their bodies. This has been a book about body alienation—feeling that one's body is strange to one, merely a bundle of chemicals and water that periodically needs professional attention and maybe some supplements. We don't love our bodies because we don't love ourselves.

But there are other ways to inhabit one's body, and one's world. Although large social structures often thwart our efforts to live a decent life—think of private health care or poverty or suburban sprawl—we can make changes, affecting ourselves and the world one organic apple and three-miler at a time. One of the themes of the long-ago sixties was that individual acts of bravery, and interpersonal kindnesses, prefigure a brave and kind world. By 'prefigure' I mean help-bring-about-by-modeling—a leap from the local and personal to the global and structural. I know a guy who organizes road races for runners who want no-frills races and low entry fees. He themes his races to support various types of social justice, opposing racism, sexism, and corporate greed.

He promotes running and a better world. His activities are embryos of a future world. "Do unto others" has long been the golden rule, since the Greek philosopher Aristotle and, later, the Enlightenment philosopher Kant. But Sheehan, the philosopher of running, is also saying "Do unto yourself"; treat yourself well, disentangle from the world when the world crushes the will, and go long, becoming Emerson's good animal. Sheehan recognized that the loneliness of the long-distance runner leads runners to shun the embrace of others. Late in his life, he realized that the loneliness of the run should lead one back toward civilization—an out-and-back course leading home.

Body problems are social problems because the body has been colonized by large corporations who variously harm and heal the body. We gorge on high-fructose corn syrup and then join a gym; we visit the Golden Arches and then purchase Lean Cuisine. If all else fails, we may try surgery, either bariatric or cosmetic. These healings may achieve lasting success. More often, they are temporary fixes, and we return to the old ways. In the meantime, we spend money and risk becoming dependent on 'experts': personal trainers, dieticians, nutritionists, coaches, physicians, fashion consultants. Although making decisions based on evidence and expertise is perhaps the defining feature of modernity, we can become over-dependent, forgetting to listen to our bodies and do our own research. Ideally, we find experts who share our sense of independence and work with us democratically to change our lives and resolve our body problems. At root, many of these problems are really problems of self-esteem; we need to learn to like ourselves more and to pay less heed to the judgments of others. I personally find exercise, conceived as a playful unity of mind and body requiring large doses of oxygen, to be the best therapy for what ails me. Some call that running.

DISCUSSION QUESTIONS

1. Do you run or walk? Does it make you "high" or just tired?! Did you stick with it? If not, why not?
2. Would it be easier for you to view exercise as a dose of necessary medicine or to feel that in doing it you were playing? Has George Sheehan gone overboard in finding mystical meaning in running?!
3. The people who run ultramarathons and transcons seem quite compulsive. How could you be or become an athlete and avoid compulsion?

VI: Food Fights

The Contested Terrain of the American Dinner Plate[1]

~~~~~

When I teach food, ears perk up. My students know every weight-loss diet. They quaff almond milk, calculate their BMIs on their devices, and struggle with food addictions. Body image is gendered, as we have known since Susie Orbach published *Fat is a Feminist Issue* in the 1970s. Many women think they are overweight, hence imperfect, while men are happier with themselves, although there is now heightened body consciousness among men, who pursue cut abs and arms. My students applaud at the conclusion of the vegan video *Fat, Sick and Nearly Dead* and they buy juicers to make green kale shakes that save lives in the film.

Everyone knows that the American fast-food diet is broken. The film *Super Size Me* and Eric Schlosser's book *Fast Food Nation* have entered the mainstream. But there is still major disagreement about what to have for dinner, with two dominant competing paradigms: high carb, low fat (HCLF) and low carb, high fat (LCHF). The revision of federal food policy hasn't helped much. After two iterations of the recommended food pyramid, the food plate was introduced in 2011, which relies somewhat less on animal protein and fills the plate with three non-meat quadrants taken up by vegetables, fruit, and grains. Meat and milk are still on the agenda, but carbs are in the saddle, as they have long been for mainstream nutrition and medicine.

As a Marxist, I find it is easy to see that capitalism makes us sick with the standard Western diet of processed food and abundant sweeteners, for profit, and then heals us with various body industries, also for profit. Neocon angst over the Affordable Care Act would likely turn to hysteria if the federal government embraced veganism on health and environmental grounds. The American right to fast-food is as central as the right to bear arms, although the fast-food sandwich, with fries, is far more lethal than the handgun, as Centers for Disease Control and Prevention (CDC) mortality

---

[1] This article originally appeared on Truth-Out.org. Reprinted with permission.

data suggest. Esselstyn, Ornish, Fuhrman, and other prophets of plant-based diets, including Colin Campbell who co-authored *The China Study*, note that we would save billions in health-care costs by eating differently. Plant-based cardiology entered the mainstream with CNN's Sanjay Gupta's 2011 documentary *The Last Heart Attack*. His account features heart-patient Bill Clinton's conversion to veganism, following bypass surgery.

These are many low-fat proponents, to whom the competing paradigm, based on the Atkins diet and now **Paleo diet**, is a response, also with many adherents. Paleos blame carbs, not meat, for American illness, and they install meat and dairy products at the center of their food plate. They argue that blood glucose does not spike and crash when protein and fat replace refined carbs and grains, breaking a carb addiction that leads to the so-called metabolic syndrome, including hypertension, obesity, and diabetes.

Vegans who rely on *The China Study*'s **epidemiology** and on Esselstyn's and Ornish's clinical experience in stemming and even reversing heart disease are met by recent best-selling books such as *Grain Brain* (Perlmutter 2013) and *Big Fat Surprise* (Teicholz), whose authors contend that meat and dairy are healthier than grains, which become addictive.

This food debate, between vegans and Paleos, spills over into an equally ferocious debate about exercise. The plant-based crew, who extol the need for complex carbs from plants, favor endurance training, such as running, while the Paleos disdain "chronic cardio" as unhealthy. The research literature on running has become a battlefield, with studies supporting the health benefits of long-slow-distance and competing studies finding that more than a little endurance training causes inflammation and even cancer. Paleos praise the gym-based CrossFit, which emphasizes total body fitness, to be achieved through lifting and nothing longer than sprints. Hardcore runners, who post on LetsRun.com, disdain anti-running ideology as the easy way out.

I've been running for nearly 40 years, and, until recently, assumed that I couldn't run and race on protein and fat fumes. Although I knew intellectually that fat burns in a carbohydrate flame—and that fat metabolism is essential when carb-supplied glycogen runs out at 20 miles—I accepted uncritically the high-carb paradigm. I found support for this in exercise physiology, for example, in the book *Lore of Running* by preeminent South African running physiologist Tim Noakes (2003). Self-styled serious runners could also cite the cult classic novel *Once a Runner*:

Cassidy . . . explained that he was a runner; just an athlete, really, with an absurdly difficult task. He was not a health nut, was not out to mold himself a stylishly slim body. He did not live on nuts and berries; if the furnace was hot enough, anything would burn, even Big Macs.

We wanted to believe that anything would burn in our hot furnaces, giving us license to gorge while we ran it off.

Recently, I experimented and tried to run and live on low carbs. The first hellish week recalled the rigors of kicking caffeine cold turkey, a battle I always lose! The second week was slightly better, and in the third week, I survived a track workout. By then I was on very low carbs and rarely feeling hungry. During the fourth week, something kicked in—perhaps the shift from one metabolic pathway to another. I was suddenly able to do an effortless 64-mile week, followed by another and another. I muttered to my wife, who rolled her eyes, that running had become a hot knife through butter!

So I read around on low-carb running and found that my guru Tim Noakes had recently reversed his field on carbs. This was huge for me, because Noakes is evidence-based and not a crackpot. He was dealing with his own pre-diabetes and weight gain, and he found that running on low carbs energized him, forcing him to rethink conventional wisdom about the need for endless carbs.

My takeaway from the reading I have done and my own recent experiences on the roads is that there is genuine metabolic diversity, with some people accommodating carbs and others resisting them, perhaps for genetic reasons. As a vegan, I could accept the low-carb part of Paleo, but not the high-fat part, especially where fat is derived from animals and dairy. It is challenging to eat plants and get sufficient protein and fat to run, but not impossible, suggesting low carb, low fat as a dialectical synthesis of the warring paradigms. I knew veganism was right for me, as it is for Scott Jurek (2013) (*Eat & Run*), who won the hundred-mile Western States Endurance Run seven times in a row eating only plants.

Michael Pollan and Alice Waters offer a final perspective on cooking and eating that emphasizes the DIY pastoralism and pragmatism of the 1960s. Waters, emerging from the Berkeley 1960s', which saw the Diggers provide free food, revolutionized American cooking by founding Chez Panisse in 1971, which relies on locally sourced food. Pollan, in his recent book *Cooked*, writes from his own experience about how home cooking is more satisfying and healthier than relying on processed Big (Fast) Food. His simple admonition: "Eat Food. Not Too Much. Mainly Plants."

The United States cannot afford food capitalism, given the interaction between health-care costs and the Western diet. But as Thomas Piketty has recently shown, capitalism does not accept limits; the rich get richer—and the sick, sicker. Nearly half a century ago, feminists put bodies on the political agenda. There they remain, as we struggle over what to have for dinner.

DISCUSSION QUESTIONS

1. Based on your experience, do you believe in a standard diet paradigm that applies to everyone (for example, high carb, low fat/low carb, high fat)? Or do you believe we would be better "dialectically synthesizing" different paradigms, in order to account for metabolic diversity?

2. Have you ever made a conscious decision to cut something out of your diet (caffeine, dairy, meat, etc.)? Did you feel better physically afterwards?

VII: Vegans Who Run

B ody politics has been on the radar at least since feminists noticed that fat is a feminist issue. Earlier, Merleau-Ponty and Beauvoir contested the Cartesian splitting of mind and body. Their compatriot, Sartre, hung with them at Les Deux Magots in Paris, where existentialism, stressing personal agency, was born. Even philosophers have to eat.

Susie Orbach (1978) penned *Fat is a Feminist Issue* at a time when the women's movement was differentiating itself from, although borne of, the male New Left. Feminist theory and practice recognized that the personal is political. The so-called private sphere concealed very public and political matters, such as who does housework and childcare, how sexuality is transacted, birth control, career primacy, and the objectification and self-objectification of women's bodies. There is by now a vast literature (for example, Bordo 1993; Hesse-Biber 1996) on the specific issue of women's weight and self-esteem.

Feminist studies sprang from feminist practice, beginning with suffrage. Feminist scholarship was always in service of a personal politics, which helped women negotiate various gender troubles, from sexuality to children to dealing with men. The empowering of sixties women led to legal, economic, and cultural changes that, together, have shrunk the income gap, left women as the majority of college students, and led to women's participation in politics and sports.

In 1967, Katherine Switzer (2007), who loved to run, crashed the male-only Boston Marathon, leading to Title IX in 1972 and, eventually, to the first women's Olympic Marathon in 1984. The race director, Jock Semple, tried unsuccessfully to throw Switzer off the course. (Boston had been completed covertly by a "bandit" runner, Roberta ("Bobbi") Gibb, in 1966, when she ran the very quick time of 3:21. And Merry Lepper reportedly completed the 1963 Culver City Marathon, running unofficially.) The delirious applause awaiting the Olympic winner, Joan Benoit, as she ran into the Los Angeles Coliseum signaled that women had begun to turn their objectified bodies into powerful subjects. Maybe Joanie did not think in these terms, having grown up efficacious in Maine and perhaps not having taken women's studies courses at Bowdoin. Nevertheless, a straight line can be drawn from Switzer, Gibb, and Lepper to Benoit (1987) to the massive participation of women today in 5Ks, half-marathons, marathons, mud runs, triathlons, and nearly every other venue of athletic participation. Showing my age, I marvel at the fact that most of my women college students never knew a world before Title IX. For them, soccer, volleyball, softball, and track are unproblematic options.

When Switzer blazed the way for women in sports, Gatorade was two years old. McDonald's had not yet opened a franchise in my hometown of Eugene, Oregon, where the Bill Bowerman-coached Oregon track teams were winning national titles and Olympic medals. Bowerman had returned five years earlier from a visit to New Zealand, where he met Arthur Lydiard (Lydiard and Gilmour 1978), the father of modern endurance training theory, about whom I will speak later.

We had not yet become a fast-food nation (Schlosser 2012), with rampant body problems, stemming from inactivity, too many sugar and fat calories, processed food, factory-farmed vegetables and meat, and fried food. The worst of these body problems include heart disease, cancer, diabetes, autoimmune disorders, and obesity. We medicalize and commercialize body problems, giving rise to body industries such as mainstream health care, big pharmaceutical companies, gyms, fad diet plans and drugs, and cosmetic and bariatric surgery. The "Western diet" makes people sick and then they are healed, for profit.

And so, just as patriarchy triggered a feminist politics of the personal, making the private public and political, which in turn spurred a feminist paradigm of theory and scholarship, so a fast-food nation has triggered a personal food and body politics. I argue here that this food and exercise practice has generated a new interdisciplinary framework perhaps best called Critical Food and Exercise Studies. Here, I weave the disparate threads of this paradigm, and also argue for an appreciation of *endurance veganism* as a personal politics tying together food and exercise.

I discuss four literatures that congeal into Critical Food and Exercise Studies: critical food theory (Pollan [2007, 2008]; Schlosser [2012]; Petrini [2003]), plant-based epidemiology and cardiology (Esselstyn [2008]; Ornish [1990]; Campbell [Campbell et al. 2006]), running/endurance theory (Lydiard [Lydiard and Gilmour 1978]; Bowerman [Bowerman and Harris 1967]), and running veganism (Jurek [2013]; Roll [2012]; VanOrden [2013]). Synthesizing the four literatures above, I argue for *endurance veganism* as a personal politics appropriate to fast-food nation.

Critical Food Theory

Pollan, Schlosser, Petrini, and Moss address food Fordism in post-World War II America, which has become a global model. From within sociology, Ritzer (2012) and Glassner (2007) contribute to this perspective, although without the focus on political economy. Schlosser's *Fast Food Nation* and a series of films and videos, including the cult classics *Super Size Me*, *Forks over Knives*, *King Corn*, and *Food, Inc.* bring this argument into the mainstream, especially for young people.

Schlosser and Pollan argue that the commodification of protein, fat, and carbohydrates produce an abundance of inexpensive calories. Even though the official food pyramid has been replaced by the food plate, somewhat decentering meat, critical food theorists focus on the centrality of meat, dairy products, and grains, especially white flour, in the American diet. At issue are (a) factory-like farming and meatpacking, which drive out local independent producers, and (b) the poor nutritional quality of fatty, sugary, meaty foods that produce cravings and dependency. Critical food theorists link these trends to the overall development of capitalism, which is now going global, reflected in the proliferation of McDonald's franchises in the People's Republic of China (PRC) and in other non-Western countries.

And so these food theorists link the logic of capital with the disastrous health consequences for consumers of the Western fast-food-based diet, which produces all sorts of health deficits, such as obesity, metabolic syndrome, heart disease, diabetes, and cancer. Schlosser links the rise of fast-food with the development of the interstate highway system, both of which have grave environmental consequences. Critical food theory is, in effect, an application of a critique of capitalism to food and farming.

Plant-based Epidemiology and Cardiology

Tony Gonzalez, now playing for the Atlanta Falcons, is arguably the greatest tight end of all time. His teammates have nicknamed him "China Study" for his eating habits. He is nearly a vegan, avoiding most meat and all dairy. *The China Study* is one of the most famous epidemiological studies, tracking the eating habits and patterns of heart disease and cancer among more than 6,000 people in China. Colin Campbell, formerly at Cornell, is the American name often associated with this voluminous study undertaken by American and Chinese health scientists. Campbell and his colleagues find strong correlations between eating meat and illness, inspiring generations of Americans to give up meat and even fish and dairy.

Gonzalez is living proof that one can be healthy and avoid meat and dairy. Tight ends are big, strong, and fast. *The China Study* is perhaps the most important inspiration of a plant-based epidemiology and cardiology. *Forks over Knives* explores the methodology and findings of *The China Study*, and also highlights the clinical work of Caldwell Esselstyn, of the Cleveland Clinic. The plot line of the movie is the struggle of two fat and illness-prone guys to lose weight and eat healthier by embarking on a diet of juiced vegetables.

Esselstyn was a general surgeon at the Cleveland Clinic, where heart bypass surgery was pioneered. Esselstyn, who won a gold medal in rowing at the 1956 Olympics, lamented the fact that people's chests were being opened up for heart bypasses, preferring prevention to dangerous and costly surgery. Instead, he took 18 very sick cardiac patients and put them on strict vegan diets (and low doses of statin drugs). Astonishingly, in almost all cases, their heart disease was slowed and even reversed, suggesting that the Western diet is the cause of much heart disease—exactly the point made by Campbell and his colleagues.

Dean Ornish, a cardiologist from California, did similar research and came up with the nearly identical conclusion that a vegan diet and exercise could prevent, retard, and reverse heart disease. Both Esselstyn and Ornish derive from the pioneering work of Nathan Pritikin, a heart patient himself, who championed low-fat diets in the 1970s and 1980s. Esselstyn's son, Rip (Esselstyn 2009), an all-American swimmer at Texas and later a national-caliber triathlete, and now a firefighter in Austin, Texas, has popularized his dad's diet in books and videos. Rip prefers the term "plant-strong" to describe the diets of his firefighter colleagues and many others who went vegan, lost weight, and improved their cholesterol and blood-pressure profiles. Perhaps predictably, his branded food is now available at Whole Foods.

Running/Endurance Theory

Switzer got American women running, drawing on the legacies of Arthur Lydiard and Bill Bowerman. As noted earlier, Bowerman traveled with his track team and brought home a revolutionary approach to running and training theory, based on the work of Arthur Lydiard. Lydiard first found fame by coaching New Zealand athletes such as Peter Snell to Olympic gold in the half-mile and mile using a method of training emphasizing long, steady miles run in order to build an aerobic base, followed by strength and speed work that would sharpen the athlete for races all the way from the half-mile to the marathon. Lydiard trained Snell to run marathons, thus providing him a base of cardiac fitness that would enable him to run not only one fast lap (quarter-mile) but four or more laps. Before Lydiard, speedy milers such as Roger Bannister and John Landy only ran fast quarter-mile "intervals," for the most part neglecting longer, slower runs that would build endurance. Now, world-class Kenyan, Ethiopian, and other world athletes use one or another version of Lydiard's pioneering approach to base building followed by sharpening and then peaking. Neo-Lydiardists include Bowerman (Moore 2006), Jack Daniels (2005), Mark Wetmore (Lear 2003), Brad Hudson (2008), the Hanson brothers (Humphrey 2012) and Renato Canova (Davis 2012).

So, how far did Lydiard want his base-building runners to run? Fully 100 or more miles a week, in double daily workouts! Hard and long days would be followed by easy, recovery days, a hard/easy pattern developed by Bowerman at Oregon. But Bowerman brought back to Eugene another very powerful idea, which is, I believe, the real legacy of Lydiard: he exposed Americans to Lydiard's contention that anyone can run a marathon, anyone can become an athlete, if they proceed patiently, developing full aerobic capacity (Bowerman and Harris 1967). Not long after he returned from New Zealand, the streets of Eugene were filled with "joggers," sheer amateurs who ran alongside the elite "men of Oregon."

Bowerman helped found Nike, which introduced the Cortez and Waffle trainers and thus nearly single-handedly started the first running revolution during the 1970s and 1980s. By now, at the height of the second running revolution, races have expanded to include women, walkers, and people struggling to get into shape and lose weight. Kenneth Cooper (1977), a Dallas cardiologist, converged with Lydiard and Bowerman in his classic self-help treatise, *Aerobics*, in which he argues that people can achieve substantial fitness by doing half an hour of cardiac work at least three times a week. It is perhaps inevitable that Nike began with running shoes sold out of the back of a VW to serious runners at local races, and emerged as a global corporation that sells expensive apparel to non-athletes.

Running Veganism

As road running evolved from its early 1970s/1980s edginess—think of Oregon's iconic runner Steve Prefontaine, a rebel without a cause—to a more corporate and commodity version today, with high-fashion gear and for-profit races, rebellious runners moved away from short road races, such as 5 and 10Ks, to off-road trail races that are frequently much longer than 26.2 miles, the marathon distance. Ultra-runners are often hippies who live off the grid, subsisting on meager income and the occasional shoe-company contract. The Boulder-based Anton Krupicka comes to mind. Some ultra-runners, such as Charlie Engle and Marshall Ulrich (2011), embark on journey runs, from city to city and across whole continents. James Shapiro (1982) chronicled his own solo "transcon" (across the United States) in *Meditations from the Breakdown Lane: Running Across America*. And a Herculean 4,000 mile run across Africa was captured in the stirring movie *Running the Sahara*. A tamer, off-beat 197-mile relay from Mount Hood to the Oregon Coast is chronicled in the film *Hood to Coast*.

Scott Jurek, America's greatest ultramarathoner, grew up in the meat-eating wilds of Minnesota and discovered his distance-running talent. Eventually, he shifted to plants and gave up meat and dairy altogether, as he discussed in *Eat & Run*. When Jurek went vegan, he became a great runner, and won the fabled Western States 100-miler from Squaw Valley to Auburn, California seven times in a row. Tim Van Orden and Rich Roll are also ultramarathoners who follow a vegan diet. As they abandoned the Western diet, and derived life-giving protein, carbs, and fat from plants, their performances improved, they became leaner, and they recovered from effort more quickly. They were *endurance vegans*, supremely fit, Lydiard-trained athletes who reject factory food, fast-food, refined food as they strike a balance with nature by running lightly through it. For these runners, running, fueled by a vegan diet, was a form of critique and liberation, a politics of the personal.

*****

A body politics, stressing non-Western, plant-based diets and endurance exercise, gives people control over their own health, including their relationship to nature and animals. But it is also playful activity not done for instrumental reasons, such as achieving a certain body mass index (BMI) or getting a promotion. Kant talked of freedom as purposive purposelessness, which is very much the argument made by George Sheehan, a running cardiologist. The philosopher and poet of running, Sheehan (1978), in *Running and Being*, speaks of running, a meaningless activity, as the key to meaning, which is achieved when the mind and body mesh and move fluidly. In my (Agger 2011) writing about bodies and runners, I address the experience of flow, which involves breathing and rhythmic movement (also see Csikszentmihaly 1990).

Vegans who run protest capitalist food, transportation technologies based on the internal combustion engine, and the commodification of exercise. They resist alienated labor by spending their own sweet time on the road or trail. Sheehan argued that we are most fully human when we exercise, and now reporters on exercise–brain science such as Chris Bergland (2007) trace this to the production of endorphins, serotonin, and endocannabinoids during endurance activity, which produce what he calls bliss. This from a guy who sweated through the cruel 135-mile Badwater run across Death Valley in the summer! I rarely have a runner's high, perhaps because in my running life I teeter on the edge of overtraining. Running blunts anger and alienation, and, matched with a plant-based diet, insulates one against the toxins of the Western diet and mainstream medicine, which picks up the pieces. It is difficult to be at cross-purposes with oneself when one runs 35 to 40 miles a week or more.

This is not a jeremiad against meat or dairy. Meat is not just meat; free range is vastly different from factory fed and fattened. Vegans need B12, which may come in the form of a supplement. Pritikin and the rural Chinese view meat as a condiment. Rigidity derives from dogma. But there is no denying that non-Western cultures such as that of the Tarahumara Indians enjoy freedom from disease, longevity, and the vitality of their native trail runners. Chris McDougall (2011), who gained entrée to the Tarahumara through mystic-hippie runner Micah True ("Caballa Blanco"), introduces readers in *Born to Run* to minimally shod trail running. Ironically, True, on a long run in Utah, died at 58 of cardiac disease. He was running alone in the wilderness he loved. Running doesn't convey immortality, as other running gurus discovered. Jim Fixx (1977), who wrote *The Complete Book of Running*, died, while running, at 52, while George Sheehan died at 78 of prostate cancer, discovered during a routine exam at the Cooper Clinic in Dallas. Bill Rodgers (2013), the draft-avoiding New

England marathoner who won many Bostons and New Yorks, is beating back prostate cancer. It does not need to be said that runners are not immortal, but one notices here that heart disease and cancer are inflected by the Western diet. A physician who ran, Sheehan felt invulnerable and avoided prostate exams until it was too late.

As soon as one writes the word "runner," one imagines training schedules, shoes, running groups, and VO_2 max (oxygen uptake) testing—running reduced to dreary science and consumer goods. One can spend $1,000 a year on race entry fees if one races a lot. Races dot the bucket lists of many, who abandon the sport once they have the 13.1 sticker on their gasoline cars. By the same token, vegans often seem cultic and puritanical, and they regard less sturdy souls as morally inferior. Gyms resemble factories with work stations.

Runners, prone to compulsiveness, readily invest their—our!—avocation with metaphysical importance. Meanwhile, our bodies break down. The female athlete's triad syndrome combines eating disorders such as anorexia, osteoporosis, and amenorrhea. Some Division-I track teams have both male and female athletes keeping calorie diaries. No one is immune. I rationalize owning a Garmin Forerunner (Global Positioning System (GPS) watch), and I run Veronique Billat's (2013) trendy vVO_2 workouts. ("V" doesn't stand for vegan.) It is easy to become too invested.

Running teaches one not to be attached to the inessential. Marcuse (1964) writes of false needs. Running vegans are minimalists. Shoes, beans, broccoli, and tortillas are a runner's basic needs. Like Shapiro, I am attracted to distance because enduring distance requires one to confront oneself. It is the hard path. Haraki Murakami (2009) writes of this in *What I Talk about When I Talk about Running*, suggesting a convergence among Zen-oriented runners and the classic 1970s treatment by Pirsig (1974), *Zen and the Art of Motorcycle Maintenance*. You can't tell yourself lies when the glycogen is nearly gone, and you are running on fumes.

My favorite running writer remains Jim Shapiro, who wrote about his transcon and about an earlier six-day go-as-you-please race in England. That essay, "Swifts on the Wing," borrowed the metaphor of the swift, a bird that never touches ground. By Shapiro's telling, only the crazy few, committed to distance for its own sake, would run endless laps of a track, piling up 60 or more miles a day for six days. Few in the mainstream media tracked Charlie Engle and Marsh Ulrich's 2008 attempt to set a land speed record across America, captured in their film *Running America*. One of them couldn't finish and they didn't remain friends, showing that remorseless endurance activities don't guarantee the endurance of relationships.

It is challenging to pierce the thin boundary between personal politics and a more public kind, involving social movements, institutions, power. As the sixties fizzled out and a long siege of reaction set in, connecting Nixon/Hoover to Reagan/Bush, Jr./Rove, former activists grew dispirited and turned toward personal growth, communes, and organic farming. Jacoby (1975) lamented a politics (purely) of subjectivity and Lasch (1979) warned of a culture of narcissism. This is tricky, because feminists aptly demonstrated the connection between bedroom and boardroom, body politics and a more public kind.

Marcuse (1969) in *An Essay on Liberation* argued that radical change must pass through, and affect, the self. It must be chosen, desired. But in *Counterrevolution and Revolt* (1972) he tracked the descent of progressive personal politics of early Students for a Democratic Society (SDS) into the authoritarianism of the Weather Underground. Feminists were perhaps more adept than the male Left at joining personal politics and legislative and political-economic agendas. Endurance veganism is inadequate unless it leads to critiques and transformations of agribusiness, school lunch programs, federal farm subsidies, mainstream nutrition, and health care. Perhaps swimming upstream in a carnivorous state, the University of North Texas opened a vegan cafeteria. Courses in aerobic activities, such as running and walking, should be part of every curriculum, from K to 12 and beyond. Attention deficits are the body's responses to the microphysics of school desks and inactivity as well as the stress produced by hectoring adults. It is a national tragedy that discipline has become pharmacological as we medicate restless young bodies.

Vegans who run have the same problems as the rest of the world, except for meat, dairy, sugar, processed food, heart disease, certain cancers, diabetes, hypertension, and the stressful rat-race of alienated labor. But, as we learned during the sixties and seventies, personal politics matter, even if they are concealed by patriarchs who wanted to keep them invisible and now by big food, medicine, and pharma. Food and body politics call forth endurance veganism as a lifestyle and political stance. Critical food and exercise studies track these interesting developments, expanding sociology into exotic realms such as clinical cardiology, nutrition, agricultural political economy, and training theory. Sociologists have to eat.

DISCUSSION QUESTIONS

1. What is the relationship between capitalism, the food we eat, and the health-care industry? How do each of these sustain one another?

VIII: Coda

Toward 'Slowmodernity'

These theses summarize my argument in this book:

1. Capitalism makes us sick and then attempts to heal us with commodified (for-sale) fixes such as weight-loss diets, supplements, gymnasia memberships, even plastic surgery. Alienation affects bodies.
2. Earlier, bodies under Fordism and of course before Fordism labored under cruel conditions.
3. Now, bodies under post-Fordism don't labor enough but are squeezed into office cubicles, school desks, and automobile seats.
4. Diets based on processed food and high-fructose corn syrup (Fordism applied in agribusiness) contribute to coronary artery disease, high blood pressure, weight gain, atrophying of the joints and connective tissues.
5. Positivism purports that we can study the body objectively, from the outside, using various health indicators measured at the annual physical exam. These indicators, such as body mass index (BMI), are almost always quantitative.
6. The BMI ignores muscularity and hence discriminates against athletes, thus rewarding people who are sedentary.
7. What Pollan calls 'nutritionism' examines food in terms of its chemical and nutritional constituents and then 'enriches' food that has already been processed. There is little evidence that processed food, once enriched, is equivalent in healthfulness to the original unprocessed food.
8. The mainstream indicators of health revolve around weight, which is grounded in acceptable femininity and masculinity. There is little evidence that obesity can kill, but rather obesity is one of the side effects of the fat-laden standard American diet, eaten by largely sedentary people. Other more dangerous side effects include high cholesterol and hypertension.
9. Weight is a convenient positivist obsession because it is a single number, because the diet industry is lucrative, and because it rewards women for starving themselves, only lowering their self-esteem.
10. A nation that exercises necessarily reduces time spent in paid labor and in productive consumption.

11. To be healthy one must be fit (Emerson's 'good animal'), but fit people can be unhealthy if they are alienated from their bodies and food.

12. Consuming large quantities of oxygen while letting the body carry the mind in exercise produces the experience of flow, of mind–body unity. Descartes was probably not a runner. It took us until George Sheehan to undo Cartesian philosophy, which separates mind and body.

13. It would be revolutionary if all Americans, or as many as could, walked, ran, or cycled to and from work and school. They would view time differently; they would get exercise, burn calories, and even derive certain mystical benefits (flow); and they would certainly be happier. The eight-hour work day could shrink to six or seven in order for people to stop smell the roses on the way.

We cannot solve body problems such as obesity and heart disease without solving a host of other social problems that have impact on bodies: the organization of work, the health care system, our dependence on professionals, corporate food and agriculture, jobs that do not challenge people, our reliance on cars, the organization of cities that thwart walking, running, and biking.

As a runner, I have my peeves! Roads without shoulders, aggressive drivers, above all too much cement everywhere. Even most running/biking paths are made of concrete, which breaks the bones and causes any manner of injuries. Barefoot running strengthens the feet and forces correct foot strike, which prevents biomechanical problems and injuries. But people like the Tarahumara ran barefoot or thinly shod on trails, Mother Nature's 'sidewalks.'

An interesting trend in running, albeit only on the fringe as yet, is **trail running**. In the ten-mile trail race I mentioned earlier, I noticed a different vibe. There was no clock at the finish line and there was a distinct sense of community among runners. We talked during the race, helped each other, laughed together. As soon as we finished, the dude who organized the race shook our hands and placed a home-made ceramic medal around our necks. It was a difficult trek, up and down over rocks and roots. My goal was not to fall. I didn't, until mile eight. We ran in deep woods, glimpsing a blue lake through the autumnal trees. It was my best racing experience since my marathons 30 years ago, until I did a 15-mile *midnight* trail race this summer!

This suggests a timeworn strategy with which to combat the problems of an industrial and urban civilization: retreat to nature. I have written about a good society that blends the pre-modern and modern, borrowing the best from each. From modernity we would take literacy, science, medicine, global consciousness, human rights, **participatory democracy**. From pre-modern cultures we take reverence of nature, rural life, small communities bonded by face-to-face relations. What I call **slowmodernity** decelerates our harried modern life (or postmodern, which involves communication nearly at the speed of light), returning us to the rhythms of nature and of

Figure 8.1 Cross-country runners.
Source: Used with permission of University of Oregon digital collections.

our own heart rate. But we borrow selectively from the past, insisting on the modern values and scientific gains of the Enlightenment.

I include playful exercise in my concept of slowmodernity. In my perfect world, people would enjoy the fruits of science, technology, health care; they would have enough to eat without being stressed by debt and insecure jobs; they would have egalitarian and not authoritarian social relationships, including in the workplace; they would not be dependent on experts and on corporate providers; they would participate in solving their own problems, including body problems.

This is a general sketch of a good society. In personal terms, I offer a single example. When I take my car to the mechanic, I strap on a backpack and run home. I don't time myself or count the miles. I walk periodically. I might stop for a snack or eat and drink what I have in my pack. I don't have to rely on a ride home, wasting gas, and someone else's time. And I'm in no particular rush; I know that I will get home soon enough. I'm a pedestrian, relying on myself. But this isn't totally a back-to-nature strategy. I rely on my expert mechanic, with whom I have a long relationship, to fix what's wrong with our cars. There is blending here, borrowing from a time when people walked and ran to get places and from a modern era in which most people don't possess the skill to fix their cars. And for those who do, working on their cars can be a kind of play, as Pirsig (1974) suggests in his classic *Zen and the Art of Motorcycle Maintenance.*

Body problems are social in their causes and consequences. An unfit America is an unhealthy America, and much of this can be traced to the ways we eat, work, and transport ourselves. The sixties taught us that we need 'radical' change—change that goes to the root of things. This would be 'systemic' change, addressing large structures of family, work, war, and sexuality. But systemic change would involve ordinary people in their own liberation, rejecting the lives and roles scripted for them by corporate advertisers and producers. My running home from the car-repair place does not a revolution make. But it has revolutionary implications for the ways we free ourselves from dependence on the internal combustion engine, car travel, other people.

This was very much the spirit of the 1960s **counterculture**, which rejected technology as a panacea for all ills. The sixties, through hippies, feminists, and ecologists, gave us a body politics that endures in the two running revolutions, the organic food movement, slow food, abandonment of the medical model. Shapiro emerged from the tunnel of that tumultuous decade, which ended with dead Kennedys and the dispiriting rise of the right, and found himself on the long road home.

Much of my inspiration comes from the 1960s, when I was formed. Recently, I wrote a book, which doubled as a memoir, about the lasting impact of this transformational decade (Agger 2009). It was difficult to separate what was happening in the world from what happened to me, especially as I reckoned with the likelihood that I would be sent to Vietnam to fight a war I did not support. I worried that I was too young to write my memories, but the book dragged on as I struggled with its themes. Eventually, I was gray!

I believe it was no accident that the running revolution started in Eugene, as iconoclastic Oregonians reclaimed a personal politics of self-sufficiency and movement. Watching Bowerman's 'men of Oregon' run by my house suggested to me a strange new discipline that might be fun. I knew that these were serious guys. To pass P.E. we had to do the decathlon, giving me an early taste of the joy of running (and the perils of pole vaulting). I have never returned to Eugene since leaving for Canada in 1969. I plan to return soon when my son and I travel there to run in a road race. In a way, I've never left. Yet little will seem familiar to me. But in the haze of free association that running provokes, I may look over at him and see myself when I was a teenager and stalking the same streets, and I will wonder what he is seeing and thinking. Perhaps he will be imagining what it must have been like for me to grow up in the shadow of the bomb, to protest the war, and to come of age at a Eugene McCarthy benefit concert. This is the way that father and son inhabit the same world and feel connected. One day he may read this and want to write his own book about the events that formed him. Where for me it is running, for him it is tennis! He may tell his children about the time we spent together looking for America.

DISCUSSION QUESTIONS

1. Would you like your life to slow down somewhat? How can you make this happen?
2. Is one-organic-apple-and-three-miler-at-a-time a viable program for changing the world or is it simply a retreat from political activism?
3. Should we require kids to get more exercise in school and to eat healthier? What other changes can we as a society make in order to become healthier and happier without having Big Brother force us to do so?

References

Agger, Ben. 1989. *Fast Capitalism: A Critical Theory of Significance*. Urbana, IL: University of Illinois Press.

———. 1992. *The Discourse of Domination: From the Frankfurt School to Postmodernism*. Evanston, IL: Northwestern University Press.

———. 2002. *Postponing the Postmodern: Sociological Practices, Selves and Theories*. Lanham, MD: Rowman & Littlefield.

———. 2004. *Speeding Up Fast Capitalism: Cultures, Jobs, Families, Schools, Bodies*. Boulder, CO: Paradigm.

———. 2009. *The Sixties at 40: Leaders and Activists Remember and Look Forward*. Boulder, CO: Paradigm.

———. 2011. *Body Problems: Running and Living Long in a Fast-Food Society*. New York: Routledge.

American Society of Plastic Surgeons. 2018. *Plastic Surgery Statistics Report*. Retrieved September 28, 2018 (https://www.plasticsurgery.org/documents/News/Statistics/2016/plastic-surgery-statistics-full-report-2016.pdf).

Aronowitz, Stanley. 1992. *False Promises: The Shaping of American Working Class Consciousness*. Durham, NC: Duke University Press.

Atkins, Robert C. 1972. *Dr. Atkins' Diet Revolution: The High Calorie Way to Stay Thin Forever*. New York: David McKay Publishers.

Bell, Daniel. 1973. *The Coming of Post-Industrial Society*. New York: Basic.

Benoit, Joan (with Sally Baker). 1987. *Running Tide*. New York: Knopf.

Bergland, Christopher. 2007. *The Athlete's Way: Sweat and the Biology of Bliss*. New York: St. Martin's.

Bernstein, Lenny, and Ingraham, Christopher. 2017. *Fueled by drug crisis, U.S. life expectancy declines for a second straight year*. Retrieved September 28, 2018. (https://www.philly.com/philly/news/fueled-by-drug-crisis-us-life-expectancy-declines-for-a-second-straight-year-20171221.html)

Billat, Veronique. 2013. (http://www.billat.net/).

Biss, Eula. 2014. *On Immunity: An Inoculation*. Minneapolis, MN: Grey Wolf Press.

Bluestone, Barry, and Bennett Harrison. 1982. *The Deindustrialization of America: Plant Closings, Community Abandonment and the Dismantling of Basic Industries*. New York: Basic.

Bordo, Susan. 1993. *Unbearable Weight: Feminism, Western Culture and the Body*. Berkeley, CA: University of California Press.

Bowerman, William J., and W. E. Harris. 1967. *Jogging: A Physical Fitness Program for all Ages*. New York: Grosset & Dunlap.

Campbell, T. Colin, Thomas M. Campbell II, Howard Lyman, and John Robbins. 2006. *The China Study: The Most Comprehensive Study of Nutrition Ever Conducted and the Startling Implications for Diet, Weight Loss, and Long-term Health*. New York: BenBella Books.

Carrington, Ben, and Ian McDonald, eds. 2009. *Marxism, Cultural Studies, and Sport*. New York: Routledge.

Case, Anne, and Angus Deaton. 2015. "Rising Morbidity and Mortality in Midlife among White Non-Hispanic Americans in the 21st Century," *Proceedings of the National Academic of Sciences*, September 15, 2015. Retrieved November 12, 2015 (http://www.pnas.org/content/early/2015/10/29/1518393112.full.pdf?with-ds=yes).

Celiac Disease Foundation. 2018. "What is Celiac Disease?" Retrieved September 25, 2018 (https://www.guidestar.org/profile/95-4310830).

Cooper, Kenneth H. 1968. *Aerobics*. New York: Bantam.

———. 1977. *Aerobics*. New York: Bantam.

Csikszentmihalyi, Mihaly. 1990. *Flow: The Psychology of Optimal Experience*. New York: Harper & Row.

Daniels, Jack. 2005. *Daniels' Running Formula*. 2nd edition. Champaign, IL: Human Kinetics.

Davis, John. 2012. (http://www.runningwritings.com/2012/06/elite-marathoning-with-renato-canova.html).

Davis, William. 2014. *Wheat Belly: Lose the Wheat, Lose the Weight, and Find Your Path Back to Health*. Emmaus, PA: Rodale.

Descartes, René. 1956 [1637]. *Discourse on Method*. Indianapolis, IN: Bobbs-Merrill.

Dyer-Witheford, Nick. 1999. *Cyber-Marx: Cycles and Circuits of Struggle in High Technology Capitalism*. Urbana: University of Illinois Press.

Esselstyn, Caldwell. 2008. *Prevent and Reverse Heart Disease: The Revolutionary, Scientifically Proven Nutrition-Based Cure*. New York: Avery Trade.

Esselstyn, Rip. 2009. *The Engine 2 Diet: The Texas Firefighter's 28-Day Save-Your-Life Plan that Lowers Cholesterol and Burns Away the Pounds*. New York: Wellness Central.

Ewen, Stuart. 1976. *Captains of Consciousness: Advertising and the Social Roots of the Consumer Culture*. New York: McGraw-Hill.

Fixx, Jim E. 1977. *The Complete Book of Running*. New York: Random House.

Fjellman, Steve. 1992. *Vinyl Leaves: Walt Disney World and America*. Boulder, CO: Westview.

Glassner, Barry. 2007. *The Gospel of Food: Everything You Think You Know about Food Is Wrong*. New York: Ecco.

Gottdiener, Mark. 2001. *The Theming of America: American Dreams, Media Fantasies and Themed Environments,* 2nd edition. Boulder, CO: Westview.

Gouldner, Alvin W. 1970. *The Coming Crisis of Western Sociology*. New York: Avon.

Harvey, David. 1989. *The Condition of Postmodernity*. Oxford: Blackwell.

Henderson, Joe. 1969. *Long Slow Distance: The Humane Way to Train*. Mountain View, CA: Tafnews Press.

———. 1976. *The Long Run Solution*. Mountain View, CA: World.

Health Impact News. 2015. "CDC Caught Hiding Data Showing Mercury in Vaccines Linked to Autism." Retrieved November 16 (http://healthimpactnews.com/2014/cdc-caught-hiding-data-showing-mercury-in-vaccines-linked-to-autism/).

Hesse-Biber, Sharlene Nagy. 1996. *Am I Thin Enough Yet? The Cult of Thinness and the Commercialization of Identity*. New York: Oxford University Press.

Hudson, Brad (with Matt Fitzgerald). 2008. *Run Faster from the 5K to the Marathon: How to Be Your Own Best Coach*. New York: Broadway Books.

Huizinga, Johan. 1950. *Homo Ludens: A Study of the Play-Element in Culture*. Boston: Beacon.

Humphrey, Luke (with Keith and Kevin Hanson). 2012. *Hansons Marathon Method: A Renegade Path to Your Fastest Marathon*. Boulder, CO: VeloPress.

Jacoby, Russell. 1975. *Social Amnesia: A Critique of Conformist Psychology from Adler to Laing*. Boston MA: Beacon.

Johnston, Josee, and Shyon Baumann. 2009. *Foodies: Democracy and Distinction in the Gourmet Foodscape*. New York: Routledge.

Jurek, Scott. 2013. *Eat & Run: My Unlikely Journey to Marathon Greatness*. Boston, MA: Houghton Mifflin Harcourt.

Kay, Jane Holtz. 1997. *Asphalt Nation: How the Automobile Took Over America and How We Can Get It Back*. New York: Crown.

Kellner, Douglas. 1995. *Media Culture: Cultural Studies, Identity, and Politics Between the Modern and the Postmodern*. New York: Routledge.

Kiernan, Paul. 2018. "Inflation Is Eating Away Worker Wage Gains," *The Wall Street Journal*, July 12. Retrieved September 25, 2018 (https://www.wsj.com/articles/u-s-consumer-prices-increase-at-fastest-annual-rate-since-2012-1531398709).

Laing, R. D. 1967. *The Politics of Experience*. New York: Pantheon.

Lasch, Christopher, 1979. *The Culture of Narcissism: American Life in an Age of Diminishing Expectations*. New York: Norton.

Lauter, David. 2015. "Poll: Uneasy Feelings Loom over American Voters," *Missoulian*, November 9: A3.

Lear, Chris. 2003. *Running with the Buffaloes: A Season Inside with Mark Wetmore, Adam Goucher and the University of Colorado Men's Cross-Country Team*. Guilford, CT: Lyons Press.

Leiss, William. 1976. *The Limits to Satisfaction: An Essay on the Problem of Needs and Commodities*. Toronto: University of Toronto Press.

Lydiard, Arthur. 1978. *Running the Lydiard Way*. Mountain View, CA: World Publishers.

Lydiard, Arthur, and Garth Gilmour. 1978. *Running the Lydiard Way*. Mountain View, CA: World.

Lyotard, Jean-François. 1984. *The Postmodern Condition: A Report on Knowledge*. Minneapolis: University of Minnesota Press.

Marcuse, Herbert. 1955. *Eros and Civilization*. New York: Vintage.

———. 1964. *One-Dimensional Man*. Boston, MA: Beacon.

———. 1969. *An Essay on Liberation*. Boston, MA: Beacon.

———. 1972. *Counterrevolution and Revolt*. Boston, MA: Beacon.

Marmot, Michael. 2015. *The Health Gap: The Challenge of an Unequal World*. London: Bloomsbury.

Marx, Karl, and Friedrich Engels. 2002. *The Communist Manifesto*. New York: Penguin.

McDougall, Christopher. 2009. *Born to Run: A Hidden Tribe, Superathletes, and the Greatest Race the World Has Never Seen*. New York: Knopf.

———. 2011. *Born to Run: A Hidden Tribe, Superathletes, and the Greatest Race the World has Never Seen*. New York: Vintage.

McNall, Scott. 2018. *Cultures of Defiance and Resistance: Social Movements in 21st Century America*. New York: Routledge.

Mercola, Joseph M. 2014. "Truth about a 40-Year Long Cover-Up of Laetrile Cancer Treatment," October 18. Retrieved September 25, 2018 (https://articles.mercola.com/sites/articles/archive/2014/10/18/laetrile-cancer-research-cover-up.aspx).

Merton, Robert K. 1957. *Social Theory and Social Structure*. Glencoe, IL: Free Press.

Mills, C. W. 1959. *The Sociological Imagination*. New York: Oxford University Press.

Montgomerie, Tim. 2015. "A Fading Faith in Capitalism," *The Wall Street Journal*, November 7–8: C3.

Moore, Kenny. 2006. *Bowerman and the Men of Oregon*. New York: Rodale.

———. 2006. *Bowerman and the Men of Oregon: The Story of Oregon's Legendary Coach and Nike's Co-founder*. Emmaus, PA: Rodale.

Moss, Michael. 2013. *Salt Sugar Fat: How the Food Giants Hooked Us*. New York: Random House.

Murakami, Haruki. 2008. *What I Talk About When I Talk About Running*. New York: Knopf.

———. 2009. *What I Talk about When I Talk about Running*. New York: Vintage.

Noakes, Tim. 2003. *Lore of Running*, 4th edition. Champaign, IL: Human Kinetics.

O'Connor, Patrick, and Janet Hook. 2015. "Poll Finds Anger at Political System," *The Wall Street Journal*, November 4: A6.

Oliver, Eric. 2006. *Fat Politics: The Real Story Behind America's Obesity Epidemic*. New York: Oxford University Press.

O'Neill, John. 1972. *Sociology as a Skin Trade*. New York: Harper & Row.

———. 1987. *Five Bodies: The Human Shape of Modern Societies*. Ithaca, NY: Cornell University Press.

Orbach, Susie. 1978. *Fat is a Feminist Issue: The Anti-Diet Guide to Permanent Weight Loss*. New York: Paddington.

Ornish, Dean. 1990. *Dr. Dean Ornish's Program for Reversing Heart Disease: The Only System Scientifically Proven to Reverse Heart Disease Without Drugs or Surgery*. New York: Random House.

Osler, Tom. 1980. *Ultramarathoning*. Englewood Cliffs, NJ: Prentice-Hall.

Parsons, Talcott. 1951. *The Social System*. Glencoe, IL: Free Press.

Peale, Norman Vincent. 1996. *The Power of Positive Thinking*. New York: Ballantine.

Perlmutter, David. 2013. *Grain Brain: The Surprising Truth about Wheat, Carbs, and Sugar Your Brain's Silent Killers*. Boston: Little Brown. See also his website (http://www.drperlmutter.com/about/grain-brain-by-david-perlmutter/).

Petrini, Carlo. 2003. *Slow Food: The Case for Taste*. New York: Columbia University Press.

Pfeffer, Fabian T., Sheldon Danziger, and Robert F. Schoeni. 2013. "Wealth Disparities before and after the Great Recession," *Annals of the American Academy of Political and Social Sciences*, 650(1): 98–123. Retrieved September 24, 2018 (https://www.ncbi.nlm.nih.gov/pmc/articles/PMC4200506/).

Pirsig, Robert M. 1974. *Zen and the Art of Motorcycle Maintenance.* New York: Bantam.

———. 1974. *Zen and the Art of Motorcycle Maintenance: An Inquiry into Values.* New York: Morrow.

Pollan, Michael. 2006. *The Omnivore's Dilemma.* New York: Penguin.

———. 2007. *The Omnivore's Dilemma: A Natural History of Four Meals.* New York: Penguin.

———. 2008. *In Defense of Food: An Eater's Manifesto.* New York: Penguin.

Popkin, Barry. 2009. *The World is Fat.* New York: Avery.

Public Health. 2015. "Understanding Vaccines." Retrieved November 16, 2015 (http://www.public health.org/public-awareness/understanding-vaccines/vaccine-myths-debunked/).

Rapoport, Michael, and Theo Francis. 2018. "Buybacks Dress Up Profits," *The Wall Street Journal,* September 24: B9.

Ritzer, George. 2004. *The McDonaldization of Society.* Thousand Oaks, CA: Pine Forge.

———. 2012. *The McDonaldization of Society.* 7th edition. Los Angeles: Pine Forge.

Rodgers, Bill (with Matthew Shepatin). 2013. *Marathon Man: My 26.2 Mile Journey from Unknown Grad Student to the Top of the Running World.* New York: Thomas Dunne.

Roll, Rich. 2012. *Finding Ultra: Rejecting Middle Age, Becoming One of the World's Fittest Men and Discovering Myself.* New York: Crown.

Schlosser, Eric. 2002. *Fast Food Nation: The Dark Side of the American Meal.* New York: Perennial/ Harper Collins.

———. 2012. *Fast Food Nation: The Dark Side of the All-American Meal.* New York: Mariner.

Seligman, Martin. 2002. *Authentic Happiness: Using the New Positive Psychology to Realize Your Potential for Lasting Fulfillment.* New York: Free Press.

Selye, Hans. 1956. *The Stress of Life.* New York: McGraw-Hill.

———. 1974. *Stress Without Distress.* Philadelphia: Lippincott.

Shapiro, James E. 1982. *Meditations from the Breakdown Lane: Running Across America.* New York: Random House.

Shapiro, James. 1983. *Meditations from the Breakdown Lane: Running Across America.* New York: Houghton Mifflin.

Sheehan, George. 1978. *Running and Being.* New York: Simon & Schuster.

———. 1978. *Running and Being: The Total Experience.* New York: Random House.

———. 1996. *Going the Distance: One Man's Journey to the End of His Life.* New York: Villard.

Shorter, Edward. 1975. *The Making of the Modern Family.* New York: Basic.

Sinclair, Upton. 2006. *The Jungle.* New York: Penguin.

Smith, Adam. 2003 [1776]. *The Wealth of Nations.* New York: Bantam Classic.

Smith, Emily B. 2015. "Forgo the Guilt, Practice Mindful Eating for the Holidays," *Missoulian,* November 10: C1–2.

Spurlock, Morgan. 2005. *Don't Eat This Book: Fast Food and the Supersizing of America.* New York: Putnam.

Switzer, Katherine. 2007. *Marathon Women: Running the Race to Revolutionize Women's Sports.* New York: Carroll and Graf.

Taylor, Frederick. 1988. *The Principles of Scientific Management.* Mineola, NY: Dover.

Tucker, Ross, Jonathan Dugas, and Matt Fitzgerald. 2009. *Runner's World. The Runner's Body: How the Latest Exercise Science Can Help You Run Stronger, Longer and Faster.* New York: Rodale.

Ulrich, Marshall. 2011. *Running on Empty: An Ultramarathoner's Story of Love, Loss, and a Record-Setting Run Across America.* New York: Avery.

U.S. Department of Labor. 2018. "Bureau of Labor Statistics." Retrieved September 24, 2018 (https://www.bls.gov/cps/lfcharacteristics.htm#emp).

Van Orden, Tim. 2013. www.runningraw.com.

Visco, Katie. 2010. Retrieved May 10, 2010 (http://www.paveyourlane.com).

Weil, Andrew. 2006. "Richard Davidson," *Time,* April 30. Retrieved May 1, 2010 (http://www.time.com/time/magazine/article/0,9171,1187248,00.html).

Glossary/Index

~~~~~~~~~~~~~~~

Note: Page numbers followed by 'f' refer to figures.

Bannister, Roger 39

barefoot running: a trend among runners who reject overengineered running shoes in favor of running barefoot or in Vibram Five Fingers or Nike Frees in order to return to the natural footstrike of primitive runners such as the Tarahumara 47, 65

bariatric surgery: surgery such as lap-band designed to reduce food intake by downsizing the stomach, thus contributing to weight loss 32, 50

Barkley ultramarathon 43

binge eating: eating done quickly and in large volume (a whole container of ice cream!) in order to reduce anxiety and stress 24

blood-pressure, high
  see **hypertension**

blue-collar factory labor: work characteristic of 18th and 19th century industrial society that involved physical labor sited in urban factories and typically unionized 4

body image 52

body industries: for-pay industries such as gyms and fashion that address people's perceived body problems, such as being overweight 18, 19, 57
  and the body as a commodity 27–28
  failure of 25
  fashion 33–35
  salon treatments 33
  seeking to heal bodies 25–26, 28, 50
  surgery 32, 33, 50
  weight-loss 21–22, 25, 30–32
  see also gyms

body mass index (BMI): a formula measuring weight and height designed to classify people as normal weight, overweight or, occasionally, underweight 22–24, 64
  failure to measure 'muscularity' 23

body problems: issues confronted by people in calorie-abundant societies such as obesity, high-blood pressure, and lack of fitness 6, 9–11, 57
  as sociological outcomes of shifts and trends in social structure 7, 50, 65, 67

body sciences: approaches such as medicine and nutrition, practiced by credentialed experts, designed to address body problems 17
  annual physicals 20–21
  see also **body mass index (BMI)**; **medical model**; **nutritionism**

body work: methods of self-care that include exercise, dieting and sometimes even surgery as ways of improving the appearance, health and functioning of the body 33, 37–38

Born to Run 42

Bowerman, Bill 13–16, 57, 59–60
Bowerman and the Men of Oregon 14–15
breast augmentation 32
bulimia: an eating disorder that involves eating and then purging (vomiting) in order to ensure that weight is not gained 24
Burleson, Dyrol 14, 15f

C
caloric deficit: consuming an insufficient amount of calories to survive 9
caloric equilibrium: eating just enough that calories taken in equal calories expended in work, exercise, and movement 9
caloric surplus: taking in more calories than one burns off in work, exercise, and movement, leading to weight gain 9
    capital: productive wealth that creates additional wealth (e.g., investments) 6, 27
Campbell, Colin 58–59
capitalism: an economic system based on the right of people and corporations to own capital (productive wealth) and to profit from it 3–4, 27, 52, 54, 58, 64
    food capitalism 54
celebrities 31, 32, 34–35
cholesterol, high 22, 23, 27
    Liptor advertisements 23–24
A Christmas Carol 28
cardiology, plant-based 58–59
China Study, The 53, 58
commodification: putting a price on all good and services, from labor to tennis rackets to therapy 26, 45, 64
    of the body 25–26, 27, 28
Comte, Auguste 17
Cooper, Kenneth 12–13, 14
Cooked 54
cosmetic surgery: surgery designed to alter and improve one's physical appearance or correct perceived flaws 32, 33
counterculture: 1960s hippies who opposed technology, industry, and urban sprawl, preferring a back-to-nature approach to living and sometimes choosing recreational drugs 67
crash diet: a weight-loss approach that radically reduces calories ingested in order to achieve substantial short-term weight loss 22, 25, 31
credentialism: the requirement that people possess certain educational credentials (e.g., BA, MBA) in order to be hired and promoted in white-collar careers 4

Eisenhower, Dwight 7

empiricism: an approach to knowledge promoted by the Enlightenment that uses sense experience such as direct observation, often accompanied by the scientific method 3

Engels, Friedrich 27

Engle, Charlie 48, 49, 50

endurance theory 59–60

endurance training 53

endurance veganism 57, 63

Enlightenment, the: an intellectual movement begun in the 1600s that sought knowledge based on direct observation of the world and grounded in the scientific method 2, 3, 18

epidemiology: the study of patterns, causes, effects, and distributions of diseases among certain populations 53, 58–59

Esselstyn, Caldwell 58–59

Esselstyn, Rip 59

Eugene, Oregon 13, 14, 33

exercise

as body work or play 14, 37–38

invention of 9, 11, 12–15

walking as 38–40

exercise debate 53

F

false needs: Herbert Marcuse's term for perceived needs (or "wants") promoted by advertising in order to maintain a high level of consumption in post-World War II capitalism 28

False Promises 6

fashion 33–35

fashionista: a person who stays current with the latest fashions and places a high value on dressing in style 34

fast food diet 7, 11, 36, 52, 57, 58

Fast Food Nation 7

Fat is a Feminist Issue 56

Fat Politics 22

femininity: a presentation of women's sexual identity, including adornment and dress, that is grounded in the idea that women and men are fundamentally different in their sensibility and needs 31, 32, 33

feminism 56

H

hair care 33

haute couture: high fashion, with high-priced designer clothing 34

health care 36

health considerations 57, 58, 59

heart disease 9, 11, 20, 32, 65

heart-rate monitors 39

Hesse-Biber, Sharlene 32

high carb paradigm 52, 54

high-fructose corn syrup: syrup derived from corn; this sweetener is much less expensive than cane sugar and is found in many foods eaten regularly by Americans 6

Homo Ludens 38

Huizinga, Johan 38

hypertension: high blood pressure, stemming from lifestyle and diet factors and sometimes from hereditary factors 10, 22, 25, 32, 46

    medication 21

    and obesity 22, 23

hyponatremia: water intoxication, which can be life-threatening, increasingly experienced by long-distance runners in races where runners are advised to drink, drink, drink, regardless of thirst 46

I

Industrial Revolution: the emergence of the factory system and cities in Europe, England, and then the Americas beginning in the 18th century 2 phases of 3–5

injuries

    preventing 39, 45, 47

    transcon runners 49–50

    treating the demedicalized body 20, 36

Internet 5, 9

intervals: short bursts of anaerobic (without oxygen) running, followed by either walking or jogging rest, designed to make the runner faster, improve running efficiency, and accustom the runner to racing on the red line between aerobic and anaerobic exertion 13, 39

J

jogging: Bill Bowerman's term for long-distance running performed at an easy conversational pace, probably about 60 to 70 percent of maximum effort (heart rate) 12, 13–16

The Jungle 6

Jurek, Scott 60

L

M

media culture: Doug Kellner's term for a popular culture largely defined and saturated by the electronic media, such as television, movies, and the Internet 26, 28

medical model: R. D. Laing's term for viewing human problems, especially of the psyche and body, in terms of medical science, with healing prescribed by all knowing physicians or therapists 17–19
    alternatives to 36, 37, 67
    and annual physical 20–21
    de-emphasis of mind–body unity 21–22
    limitations of 19–20

meditation 44

Meditations from the Breakdown Lane 47

metabolic set point: the rate at which the body burns fuel (calories), subject to being sped up by exercise 31

Mills, C. Wright 1, 18

mind–body unity
    see **flow**

modernity: a historical period stretching from the Enlightenment to the present stressing industry, health care, literacy, democracy, and civil rights 2, 3–8, 50, 65
    health problems created by 11, 37

Moore, Kenny 14

morbid obesity: the condition when one is so overweight that one's weight itself becomes a health risk factor 24

Murakami, Haruki 41

N

nail care 33

New Left: 1960s social movements including the anti-Vietnam War movement, civil rights movement, and women's movement 11

Nike Company 15, 28, 29

Noakes, Tim 53, 54

nutritionism: a view of food and the body that recommends additives and supplements such as vitamins to ensure that people's dietary needs are met 18, 24–26, 64

O

Obama, Barack 36

obesity 22–24, 64, 65

Oliver, Eric 22–23

Olympics 23, 24, 28

Once a Runner 53

professionalism: a view that problems should be solved by experts (e.g., doctors, lawyers) who possess certain educational credentials and adequate training 20

PRs (personal records): the fastest times a runner has run in races 38

R

relative rest: an approach to rehabbing injuries, including overtraining, where one reduces one's exercise load without shutting down altogether 39

resting heart rate: the heart rate taken early in the morning or when a person is quiet and in repose 23, 39

Ritzer, George 7

routinization: Max Weber's term for the tendency of behaviors in a modern industrial society to become repetitive and governed by certain established protocols 5

runner's high: a feeling of well-being, even euphoria, achieved by some runners well into the run 44

running 13–16, 53–54, 60, 61–62
    in aboriginal cultures 42–44
    and being 40–42
    combined with walking 40, 42, 43, 48
    as exercise or play 15, 37–38
    fuel for 46
    unity of mind and body 44–45
    women's increased involvement in 38–39, 56

Running and Being 40

running economy: how efficiently runners use oxygen 19

running shoes 15, 29, 45, 46–47

running/endurance theory 59–60

running veganism 60–61, 62

Running the Lydiard Way 13

Running the Sahara 48

S

salon treatments 33

Schlosser, Eric 7, 58

scientific management: Frederick Taylor's term for a managerial model grounded in time-and-motion studies that maximize workers' productivity 3, 17

second running revolution: an upsurge of mass interest in running from the 1990s to the present, where the most popular races are the 5K and half marathon 29, 38–39, 41

self-esteem: one's sense of self-worth, how one views oneself 31, 34, 50

Shapiro, James 47–49

Sheehan, George 40–41, 43, 45, 50, 65

Shorter, Frank 14

Sinclair, Upton 6

Slow Food 25

slowmodernity: my term for a blending of pre-modern rural life based on regular physical activity with the benefits of modernity, such as health care and science 65–66

Smith, Adam 6, 27

Snell, Peter 13

sociology: the academic discipline founded by Auguste Comte in the 19th century that examines the social causes and consequences of organized group behavior 1, 17–18

speed work: fast running, performed once or twice a week designed to sharpen the runner after weeks of long-slow-distance base building (usually done from 85 percent to 100 percent of one's aerobic capacity) 13, 39, 44–45

sport, professionalization of 29

sports-clothing industry 29

sports drinks 46

Standard American Diet (SAD): Americans' contemporary diet heavily reliant on fatty, sugared, salty processed foods 7

stress 10–11, 21

supplements: vitamins such as D and B-complex added to one's diet in order to enhance a diet consisting mainly of processed food 24, 25

surgery 32, 33, 50

T

Tarahumara 42–43, 47, 61

Taylor, Frederick 3

telecommmuting: working from home, from the car, or anywhere outside of the traditional office cubicle 5

tempo running: quick but not anaerobic running, usually interspersed in a long-slow-distance effort that raises the heart rate no higher than 85 percent of capacity 39

theming: the national and global franchising of food, hotels, and entertainment that have certain identifiable common themes (or 'brands'), such as Disney World 7

trail running: running and racing on soft and wooded trails, often single-track, as an alternative to running on the roads and track 42, 43f, 46, 65

training effect: the level of exertion in exercise at which one stresses the cardiovascular system sufficiently that it becomes stronger 12–13, 39, 40

transcon: runs across a continent, from coast-to-coast 29, 47–50

U

Ulrich, Marshall 48

ultramarathons (ultras): organized races, conducted on the roads or on trails, beyond the standard marathon distance of 26.2 miles, with 50- and 100-milers being common distances 40, 42–43, 60–61

V

vanity sizing: labeling clothes as a size smaller than they actually are in order to flatter the wearer 33

Visco, Kate 48, 49, 50

veganism 52–53, 54, 58–59, 60–61, 62, 63

VO$_2$ Max: a measure of oxygen uptake, monitored on a treadmill as one breathes during exercise 18–19

W

walking 7–8
    combined with running 40, 42, 43, 48
    as exercise 38–40

Weber, Max 5

weight lifting 23, 30, 31

weight loss 21–22, 25, 30–32

wellness: an approach to health that preempts health problems and illness through preventive strategies such as exercise and diet 21

Western diet 52, 54, 58

Wetmore, Mark 39–40

What I Talk About When I Talk About Running 41

white-collar office work: work, usually of a professional and service-providing kind, performed in corporate office buildings often divided into cubicles 4–5

'whole foods' 24–25

women and sport 56–57

Z

Zahab, Ray 48

zone: a feeling of flow and mind–body unity during exercise when the body seems to have a mind of its own and performs effortlessly 37, 44